NEW MEXICO'S
STOLEN LANDS

A HISTORY OF RACISM, FRAUD & DECEIT

RAY JOHN DE ARAGÓN

Published by The History Press
Charleston, SC
www.historypress.com

Copyright © 2020 by Ray John de Aragón

All rights reserved

Front cover, top: author's collection; *bottom*: photo by Rosa María Calles, 2018. *Back cover*: author's collection; *inset*: unknown photographer, circa 1945. Author's collection.

First published 2020

Manufactured in the United States

ISBN 9781467144032

Library of Congress Control Number: 2019951841

Notice: The information in this book is true and complete to the best of our knowledge. It is offered without guarantee on the part of the author or The History Press. The author and The History Press disclaim all liability in connection with the use of this book.

All rights reserved. No part of this book may be reproduced or transmitted in any form whatsoever without prior written permission from the publisher except in the case of brief quotations embodied in critical articles and reviews.

Dear Ray: As they say in Spain, to the matador at that moment when the bull first comes into the ring through the toril gate: ¡Suerte chamaco!
—John Nichols, author of The Milagro Beanfield War

Ray John de Aragón has done his homework, legwork, and spadework a historian needs to do to get to the truth.
—Sabine Ulibarrí

This book is dedicated to the unique and wonderful Hispano history, heritage, culture and traditions of New Mexico. This area has its own centuries-old culture, dating from 1598, when early Spanish colonizers settled it. The vibrant traditional and contemporary Hispano visual arts, dances and music of New Mexico are recognized worldwide and are equal to the native cultures of Mexico, South America, Central America, Puerto Rico and Cuba. Our story has not often been factually or historically accurately told. Hispanic New Mexicans have blazed trails in all walks of life, have made marvelous impacts on the history of the United States and have paved the way for other Latinos to follow for many generations, with nationally and internationally recognized political and governmental leaders such as Padre Don Antonio José Martínez, New Mexico's folk hero priest; U.S. senator Dennis Chavez; and U.S. senator Joseph M. Montoya. They made it much easier for Latinos from other areas in the United States to follow. At one time, New Mexico was called the Territory of Santa Fe. This is why the capital city of Santa Fe was so widely known in the Spanish world. Hopefully, this book will aid in having New Mexico's history much better recognized and more appreciated by all Americans.

CONTENTS

Acknowledgements	9
"Onofre Romero," by S. Omar Barker	11
Introduction: Historical Setting	13

I. Settlement and Sacrifice

1. A Spanish Royal Grant	23
2. Seeds of Land Struggles	37
3. Shadows of Theft	63

II. Disenchantment in New Mexico

4. A Confederate Invasion	69
5. Contrast in Lands	79
6. Moved by Greed	100
Bibliography	125
About the Author	128

ACKNOWLEDGEMENTS

I wish to acknowledge Doña Fabiola Cabeza de Baca, who recollected life on the Llano Estacado, the Staked Plains, and always talked glowingly about her family's past on those ancient lands that were lost. Even at an advanced age, she smiled while remembering stories about her family and friends farming and ranching on those lands. She tremendously impressed me. The "Golden Orator," Dr. Sabine Ulibarrí, while remembering his past in Tierra Amarilla, the lands of his family, said he was passing the torch to me toward the end of his fantastic life. I was overwhelmed by his most beautiful words. I have strived to do him justice.

I have always also greatly appreciated Fray Angélico Chávez, whom my father, Maximo de Aragón, wanted to introduce me to at the fray's parish church in Cerrillos, New Mexico, when I was eleven years old. "This is your cousin," my father said. I beamed with pride and joy, especially when Fray Angélico gave me one of his books and inscribed it, "To my little cousin." My father, who always kept up with history, and my mother, Cleofas Sánchez de Aragón, both of whom were my mentors, said when I was seventeen years old, "You need to join the Alianza, led by Reies López Tijerina." I did, and I was always impressed by Tijerina's charisma, photographic memory and dynamic personality.

I traveled with Reies and William "Bill" Higgs, his civil rights attorney, seated quietly in the back seat of Bill's car, listening to strategy being discussed and plans being made. Reies and his wife rented my father's home in Albuquerque. There was a very close attachment, especially when Reies vociferously discussed with me the Spanish history of territorial lands and the loss of lands in New Mexico.

John Nichols was also very kind and supportive when I spoke with him in Las Vegas, New Mexico. I very graciously acknowledge everyone who has impacted me and my efforts in writing this much-needed story of our beloved Nuevo Mexico and its history.

Above: A sheepherder takes his flocks of sheep carefully around the bend at Romeroville near Las Vegas, New Mexico. *Unknown photographer, circa 1946. Author's collection.*

Right: *En Luto* (In Mourning), oil painting by Rosa María Calles shows a crying woman. Losing ancestral lands and the loss of livelihoods brought tears to the people. 1980. *Rev. Vincent Paul Chavez collection.*

Onofre Romero

*Up to the timberline, grassy and steep,
Onofre Romero goes herding his sheep,
Where the mountain's brow is scowling.
Gray burros plod with him to carry his bread—
At night the poor shepherd dog creeps to his bed,
When the timber wolves are howling.*

*He knows how to talk to the thunderstorm,
And bed down the flock where the coves are warm
When the black, black clouds are growling;
But oh, in the night when he's all alone
He hears the ghosts of the mountain groan,
And the lonely coyotes howling!*

*His woolies lie bleating in plaintive dismay—
Onofre must listen all night and all day—
Oh, an owl to the moon is crying!
Great grizzlies have come in the dead of the night
And killed his gray burros. The late moon is white,
And into the west goes dying.*

*Up into the dawn on the highest pass
Onofre goes driving his sheep to grass,
And the firs below are sighing,
For they heard, as Onofre came driving through,
The poor shepherd bleat like a frightened ewe,
And a he-goat prophesying.*

*Onofre goes up with the flocks every year,
His black eyes are wild and his talking queer—
Look! Shadow wolves, shadow wolves come creeping!
The moon of the mountains is white with woe,
And in the village far down below
A black-shawled woman is weeping.*

—S. Omar Barker, 1935, Las Vegas, New Mexico

INTRODUCTION
HISTORICAL SETTING

A little rebellion now and then is a good thing.
—*Robert F. Kennedy*

The decade of the 1960s was a period marked by racial and social unrest in the United States. Great leaders such as Martin Luther King Jr. and Cesar Chávez emerged as heroic figures that led movements directed toward human rights and equal justice. New Mexico also had a great leader, Reies López Tijerina, who led a similar movement that decried loss of lands, livelihoods and basic human dignities. Inspired youth and adults in other states who took up Tijerina's standard of leadership spread from New Mexico to other states in the Southwest, including California, Arizona, Colorado and Texas, where Tijerina had worked as a Presbyterian minister. Out of the struggles and ashes of human despair, people rose up to fight and animate the national American scene with cries of American hopes and dreams. This is the story of New Mexico, which found itself in endless tears brought out in all citizens who were caught up in the fraud and deceit of opportunism, loss of lands and trampling of justice. During the zeal and fervor of this dynamic period in American history, the populace rose up in New Mexico to fight for democracy and its founding principles.

It can be said that the framework, groundwork and stones placed in the loss of lands in New Mexico and the Spanish Southwest were laid in the early nineteenth century. Immigration to the Spanish territories by foreigners from the United States and other areas such as Canada and Europe steadily grew with the trade in furs, foodstuffs and other commodities. It was all a

Introduction

question of economics, with benefits to be reaped by everyone involved. Those placed at a disadvantage were the Native Americans, although the Spanish government counted them as Spanish citizens with equal rights to all Spanish citizens. The English and later American governments, in contrast, vehemently maintained that Indians had no rights, especially when it came to lands. Indian lands were subject at all times to takeover for the good and benefit of English and American citizens. It was maintained the Native Americans were ignorant as to the riches and the wealth of lands that were under their feet, which should be relished for the good of the people as a whole. These people, it was argued, should be able to colonize and settle those lands and take advantage of its metals, minerals and natural resources.

Americans, Canadians and others entering Spanish territories very quickly saw the advantages and opportunities open to them. Since Spanish women could inherit lands and English and American women could not, this paved the way to a richer future. Many American men married into wealthy Spanish families in which there were only daughters. Dowries most often included land and livestock. Therefore, American men automatically controlled those lands. In New Mexico, famous names such as Christopher "Kit" Carson, Charles Bent and others followed in this vein.

After Mexican independence from Spain around 1821, Mexican policies were more open than those espoused by the previous Spanish government as to the settlement of its territories and the granting of lands, especially to foreigners if they became naturalized Mexican citizens and renounced their previous citizenships. In Texas, Stephen F. Austin received a grant in 1827. There was also a Burnett's Grant, a Whelan's Grant, a Feisolas Grant, an extensive Cameron's Grant, an Austin and Williams Grant, De Witt's Grant and colony and a McMillan and McClones Grant. The only Spanish name appearing on a map of Texas, with parts of the adjoining states dated 1831, or 1837, was for a small grant named the de Leons Grant. Stephen F. Austin compiled the map. It was published by H.S. Tanner of Philadelphia and authorized by General Teran of the Mexican army. Austin's claim was more extensive, including a colony he was establishing. Mexican governors and high officials could grant lands for settlement. Comanche Indian lands were listed in Texas, but their lands were overrun by the other grants, since those lands had not actually been defined with set boundaries.

In New Mexico, Governor Manuel Armijo granted some lands to Americans or foreigners promising to settle and develop lands that were not previously granted to Spanish and Mexican citizens nor infringed on Indian lands. The most famous is the Beaubien Miranda Grant, issued in 1841,

Introduction

which nurtured the infamous Maxwell Land Grant, confirmed by the U.S. Congress in 1860, for 1,714,764.94 acres. This displaced entire Hispanic communities in northern New Mexico. Beaubien was a Frenchman, and Miranda was a Missourian/Spaniard turned American. Lucien Maxwell married into the Beaubien family and rapidly gained in power and influence, as did other American elite politicians, opportunists and those connected with an inner circle known as the "Santa Fe Ring."

There were many tricks of the trade used by Americans entering into New Mexico Territory, which included present-day Arizona, parts of Colorado, Nevada, Utah and even Texas. The Treaty of Guadalupe Hidalgo, signed by the United States and Mexico, officially ending the war between the two countries and guaranteed the rights of the Mexican citizens to their lands and the Native Americans to theirs. Almost immediately, land theft, fraud and deceit entered the scene. Land taxes had been virtually unknown in Mexican territorial land grants. Many of the taxes introduced were arbitrary and exorbitant.

Another trick was related to the need for surveys of the lands. It made no difference that surveyors needed no training. Anyone could be hired as a surveyor of lands. The local saloonkeeper or a passing vagrant could apply to the land office in Santa Fe, New Mexico, and be hired as a surveyor. All that was needed was a horse and a mule and the desire to travel to remote areas and look at landmarks. A measly salary prompted those who had no other recourse. This was a gold mine for monopolists to get friends and those who would be indebted to them to be hired as so-called surveyors. Therefore, those Americans claiming lands, as well as their handpicked surveyors and those controlling the government land office, had full sway when it came to confirming lands through the American Congress.

Eminent domain—the right of the government or its agents to expropriate private lands and water for public use with whatever compensation or payment is determined by the government or its agents—was another method of misappropriation of lands with little rights of the inhabitants. Homestead Acts were passed by the United States, and this allowed Americans to move into lands, develop the areas for some years and then apply for ownership. It did not make a difference that these people were applying for ownership on established lands already privately owned as individual or community grants from the Spanish and Mexican governments. Indian lands were also freely taken. In time, land grant corporations were also established wherein boards were elected from the heirs of the lands. Shares were set up for the grantees, and each grantee received a share, or shares, depending on how

Introduction

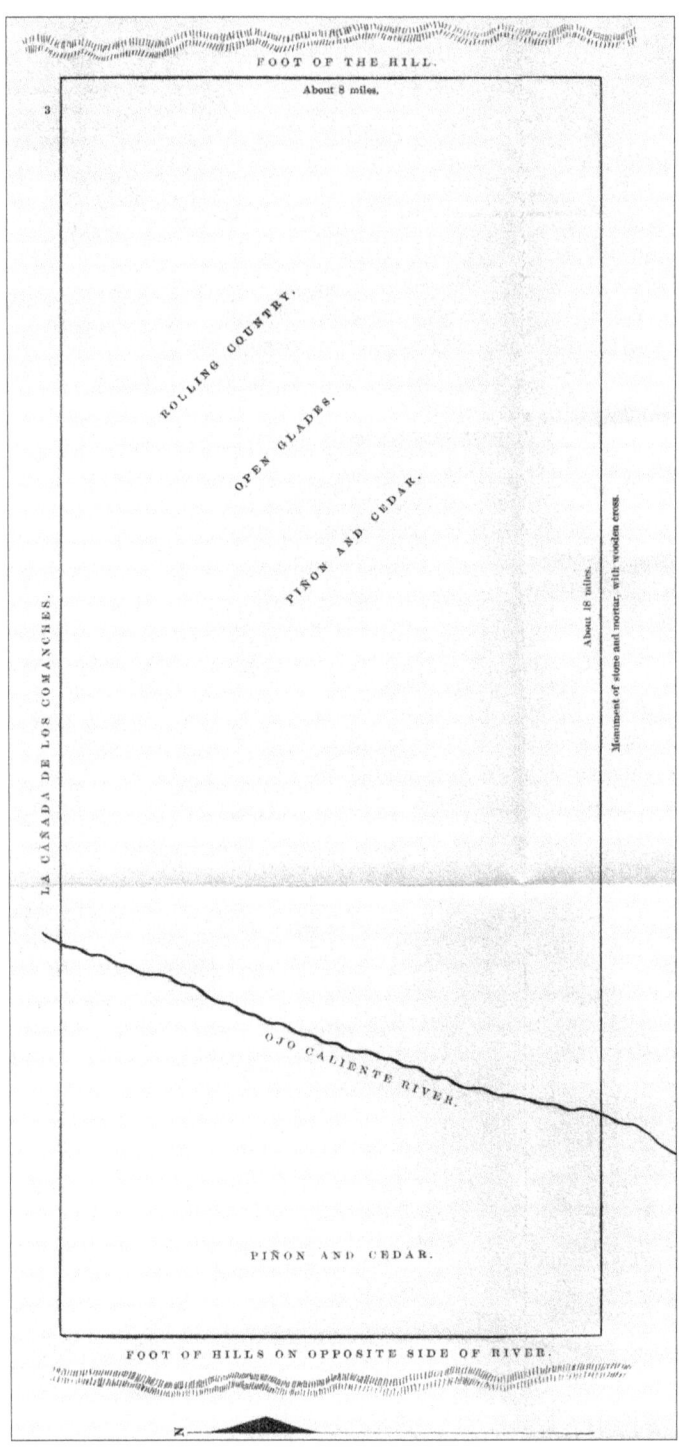

Saloonkeepers and friends of land manipulators could be surveyors. Landmarks were moved or removed to suit American claimants. This was a prescription for land theft. *Author's collection.*

Introduction

much land they developed and owned. Communal lands, owned by all, were also partitioned as shares. Shares could be bartered and sold, although this would have been highly illegal under both the Spanish and the Mexican governments. Board presidents could sell the land supposedly on behalf of the shareholders, who would receive a certain amount of money for their shares. This opened up another venue for land theft—quite often, manipulators and opportunists controlled the boards. Some land grant board representatives secured powers of attorney from heirs to provide "for their best interests" and then transferred these powers of attorney to a wealthy American or to foreign manipulators.

These land grant manipulators went by names such as the Nicolás Duran y Chávez Land Grant Company, the Tome Land Development Company and the Tierra Amarilla Land Grant Company. When lands were sold or transferred, the original heirs received little or no compensation. In fact, Native Americans received pennies on the dollar based on nineteenth-century values of properties, whereas those illegally purchasing those same lands sold them at profits based on twentieth-century values of properties. Defrauding

$2.6 Million To Be Distributed To Tome Heirs by Late November

Plans are proceeding to disburse most of $2.6 million being held in trust from the 1968 sale of the Tome Land Grant to about 3,500 heirs by late November, a court official said Tuesday.

Meanwhile, Special Master Vernon Salvador said a deadline of 4 p.m. Friday has been set for any persons wishing to claim they are heirs and are eligible for a part of the sale proceeds. Claimants must show they descend from one of about 200 grant heirs established by an 1892 court, and must have been 21 or older at the time of the sale — Nov. 4, 1968.

Salvador and officials of the First National Bank of Belen, the trustee for the sale, have been computerizing records and identifying eligible heirs. A hearing for the latest group of persons whose claims were denied has been tentatively set for Nov. 9 before District Judge Edmund H. Kase in the Bernalillo County Courthouse.

In a related matter, the court is preparing to inform about 350 former stockholders who received payments that they must repay the money. The grant, northeast of Belen, was sold for $4.7 million, and about $2.5 million was paid to the former stockholders.

A 1978 state Supreme Court ruling established that the now-defunct Tome Land and Improvement Corp. was void at the time of the sale, and ordered that the stockholders repay the money. Payments to the former stockholders varied from $8,600 to $15,000.

The Tome Land Grant received news coverage when millions of dollars were to be paid to heirs from a questionable land deal. Legitimate heirs received little or nothing. *Author's collection.*

Introduction

of lands and water resources helped to create massive landholdings for individuals—such as U.S. senator Thomas B. Catron, the largest land baron in the history of the United States, who claimed millions of acres—and for large cattle ranches, such as the Bell Ranch, which incorporated entire communities and forced people out of their homes and livelihoods. Barbed wire and hired gunmen were the rule of the day.

What did it mean for the people to lose their lands? For one thing, beloved family members who had passed on were buried on those lands. This included fathers, mothers, grandfathers, grandmothers, uncles, aunts and children. The people had sacrificed and suffered over many generations, through droughts, illness and debilitating disease. Warfare against predatory Indians, a Confederate invasion and an American invasion had also taken their tolls and inflicted pain. Daily life and a very existence would be lost through not being able to farm and ranch. Water resources were fenced in. Water was the life of the land, and this was stolen and shut off. Cattle was rustled and incorporated into large American ranches. Sheep were killed off because herding boundaries had created range wars among cattlemen and sheepherders. The Navajo Indians lost orchards of fruit trees that were intentionally destroyed; their sheep were slaughtered by Americans to take over the "Indian Country." Quite understandingly, people took to the streets to protest the loss of land.

The mid-1960s saw many protests by black Americans, Indians and Hispanics against injustice. In New Mexico, the Alianza Federal de las Mercedes (the Federal Alliance of Land Grants) rose up under the leadership of charismatic leader Reies López Tijerina. Demonstrations and marches helped to formulate the scene and bring the plight of the people to national and international attention. Indigenous and Hispanic people in New Mexico claimed that they were trying to save their land, nothing else. They had said this for generations—generations filled with pain, suffering and fear. They felt the government did not respect their lands, traditions, cultures and ways.

All of the protests, marches and demonstrations in New Mexico culminated with the famous—or infamous—Tierra Amarilla Courthouse Raid, which took place on June 5, 1967. The area of Tierra Amarilla was selected by Tijerina and the Alianza to bring the issues of injustice to national and international attention. It did get the attention, but in a negative way. The New Mexico National Guard was mobilized and went into the area with tanks and troops. The New Mexico State Police and sheriff's officers went in. Peaceful residents and demonstrators alike were handcuffed and arrested and placed into livestock corrals. The New Mexico Air National Guard was placed on alert,

Introduction

New Mexico Army National Guard troop movements into Tierra Amarilla on June 5, 1967. Land grant activists demonstrated against land theft. Chaos followed. *Unknown photographer, New Mexico Historical Society.*

and airmen equipped with riot gear were mobilized and alerted to be ready. Warmongers believed that New Mexico was on the verge of a revolution, to secede from the United States. Reies Tijerina was touted as the most hated man in America, and the most massive manhunt in the history of the United States was begun to track him down. But this would not be the first time that racism and hatred would raise its ugly head in America.

Racism has had a long history in the United States, as was seen in Selma, Alabama. Rosa Parks and others stood in the way of racism. Malcolm X, the Black Panthers, the Hispanic Black Berets, the Brown Berets and many other peaceful and militant groups were making an impact. Tijerina was arrested but then released after winning in court. But this was not enough. Robert Kennedy was murdered on June 5, 1967. James Earl Ray assassinated Dr. Martin Luther King Jr. on April 4, 1968. On May 4, 1970, the Kent State Massacre took place. The Ohio National Guard had been mobilized, activated and sent to Kent State University, where students were protesting against the bombing of Cambodia and the resultant civilian casualties. At Kent State, four students were killed and nine were wounded as guardsmen fired indiscriminately into the crowd, including those who were walking

Introduction

on sidewalks, observing what was happening. Perhaps the so-called Tierra Amarilla Courthouse Raid in New Mexico and its adverse impact had stirred up National Guardsmen. There was an attempt on the life of Reies López Tijerina when his headquarters in Albuquerque, New Mexico, was torched and ineffectually bombed.

During the turbulent era of the 1960s and '70s, which saw the deaths of Dr. Martin Luther King Jr. and Robert Kennedy and the inspiring goals of Cesar Chávez, and Reies López Tijerina, hope rose for social justice and equal opportunity for all. Out of the despair for human dignity, a cry rose up. It was a cry for educational opportunities, a cry for Hispanics and Native Americans, as well as black Americans and others, to succeed. Tijerina proposed new hope and aspirations. Hand in hand with other civil rights leaders, he touched on many issues that were unresolved. The land grant issue has a very long history. It is not only unresolved but is still also a vital problem. It is also a story that needs to be told. Many writers have skirted the major issue of land grant theft, which affects the lives of many people in New Mexico and may continue to adversely affect people for generations to come.

> *The history of Spanish and Mexican land grants and loss of Indian lands in New Mexico has been contentious, complicated and controversial. Many New Mexico state and national commissions have been established in the past to study and deal with problems of land ownership and patrimonial heritage. Unfortunately the problems involved with private, state and national disputes over many of these lands remains unresolved in New Mexico.*
> —*Governor Jerry Apodaca*

New Mexico governor Jerry Apodaca with civil rights leader Reies López Tijerina at the state capital. *Photographic Collection (#000-654-0098), CSRW, UNM Libraries.*

I
SETTLEMENT AND SACRIFICE

1
A SPANISH ROYAL GRANT

In order that our vassals may be encouraged to make discoveries and settlements in the Indies...it is our will that lands be partitioned and distributed to all those who shall go to settle new lands in towns and places which shall be assigned to them by the governor of the new settlement...and these grants may be extended and improved in a manner corresponding to the services that each grantee shall render, so as to stimulate them in the tilling of the land and rearing of cattle.
—*Philip II, King of Spain, May 25, 1596*

Spanish colonists arrived in New Mexico in 1598, leaving behind their beloved motherland but willing to endure a long, arduous journey with unknown hardships to begin a new life for themselves. Contrary to what some writers have falsely claimed and perpetuated, entire Spanish families of men, women and children arrived to start a new life in New Mexico Territory. It was a hard journey by ship and by land. Some of these very early pioneers died on the strenuous journey and were either buried at sea or on the Camino Real into New Mexico. It was a heartbreaking trip, but the indomitable colonizers were dedicated to a new life in a new land. They brought along hundreds of horses, cattle, swine and sheep, as well as thousands of seeds for fruit trees, vegetables, plant roots and flowers.

The intrepid settlers had prized belongings from their native Spain. They left beloved family members behind; knowing full well they might not, or would never, return. Trunks with jewelry and fashionable clothes were carried in wagons. At times, belongings were left by the wayside as

Don Santiago Martínez and Colonel Pascual Bailón Martínez, the brothers of famous Padre Martínez, served as witnesses on a land transfer at Taos in 1835. *Author's collection.*

a means of decreasing the weight carried in order to outrun marauding Indians who menaced the settlers. Spanish soldiers, who also brought their families, protected the caravans of settlers moving into New Mexico. These people would be given grants of lands, which had motivated them to travel on a perilous journey to begin with. Individual and community tracts of land to build homes, farms and open ranges with water and grass would be provided for everyone willing to work hard, and they would reap the rewards of the lands, which would not cross into Indian lands. It was an arrangement agreed on by the Native American tribes residing in what would be known as the Spanish Southwest.

The Spanish Roman Catholic pioneers were extremely dedicated in their Christian faith. They belonged to lay religious orders such as the Third Order of Saint Francis of Assisi, named for the patron saint of Santa Fe. They were Penitentes, or penitents, committed to the Catholic saints and commemorating the passion sufferings and death of Jesus Christ on the cross. Communities they established were dedicated to particular saints who would protect their homes and villages. Therefore, it is not very surprising that when the governor gave land grants, one of the provisions was for settlers to go to the lands and to show and demonstrate their love of these lands that they promised to care for. A promise to cherish and protect the land was done by kneeling down, scooping up the earth and kissing the dirt. In the name of God, they rose up and threw some of the soil into the air. A litany of prayers would be recited, and then the land was theirs. Spanish officials inspected the areas annually to be certain that the promises were kept and that the lands were flourishing. This process went on for centuries.

Following is an example of the granting of land from the *History of the Our Lady of Guadalupe Seminary* by the Servite priests of Belen, New Mexico (Ward Printing Company, 1930):

> *MERCED REAL. En la Villa Real de la Santa Fé de San Francisco de Asís a los quince días del mes de Noviembre de mil setecientos cuarenta, yo el teniente coronel, Gobernador y Capitán General de este Reino de la Nueva Méjico, Don Gaspar Domingo de Mendoza, visto el presente escrito por los mencionados en el, debía mandar y mande se les diese la merced que piden en nombre del Rey Nuestro Señor Que Dios Guía para que Pueblen, cultiven y beneficien para si, sus hijos, herederos, y sucesores.*
>
> *ROYAL GRANT. In the Royal City of the Holy Faith of Saint Francis of Assisi, on the fifteenth day of November, one thousand seven hundred*

and forty, I the lieutenant colonel, Governor and Captain General of the Kingdom of New Mexico, Don Gaspar de Mendoza, having seen the present petition made by the persons therein referred to, should order, that the grant be made to them of the tract they ask for, in the name of the King Our Sovereign That God Guides, in order that they may settle, cultivate, and improve the same for the benefit of themselves, their children, heirs and successors.

Don Gaspar Domingo de Mendoza noted in his book of government, on the reverse of page sixty-eight on file in the archives of the Royal City of the Holy Faith of Saint Francis of Assisi, on January 25, 1742, that he ordered and directed the senior justice of the town of Alburquerque, Don Nicolás de Chávez, to honor this new grant under the conditions and terms required. The attending witnesses were Antonio de Herrera and José Terrus. The captain general of the Kingdom of New Mexico stated that the purpose of the document was to avoid suits and difficulties at the present time as well as in the future.

Captain Don Nicolás Duran y Chávez, as the senior justice and war captain from Our Lady of Belen, had jurisdiction of the town of Alburquerque. On December 9, 1740, he gave royal possession of the grant to Captain Diego de Torres, who was serving as the representative of all persons who had petitioned for the grant. Don Nicolás stated that the decree had been published for those adjoining said lands as requested. Since there were no objections, he was honoring the petition. The decree stated:

Said lands being bounded on the north by those of Captain Don Nicolás Duran y Chávez; on the south, fronting the foundation of the house of Felipe Romero; on the west, the Puerco River; that portion on the opposite side of the river, with the boundary of the settlers of the Pure and Limpid Conception [Our Lady of Conception of Belen], *and on the east by the Sandia mountains, and on the south by the ruins and walls of the house of the aforesaid Felipe Romero; and having examined said boundaries with three attending and instrumental witnesses, according to law, I took the aforesaid Torres by the hand and walked with him over the lands, and he cried out in a loud voice, pulled up grass, threw stones, and gave other manifestations which are made and provided in such cases, receiving this possession in the name of His Majesty, quietly and peaceably, with the same boundaries contained in his petition; whereon I directed perpetual landmarks to be established, giving him lands free and with general pastures, water, watering places, timber, uses and customs, in order that he, his children, heirs, and successors, may enjoy the same without opposition, and this royal possession to be evidence of a sufficient title, and by virtue of which he shall enjoy the same as before stated, and in order that it may so appear, I placed it on record. Bernabé Baca, Baltazar Baca, and those in attendance being instrumental witnesses, who signed with me as acting judges....Attending: José Manuel Álvarez de Castillo. Guillermo Saavedra.*

Another example of the early granting of land by the Spanish government was the Miera y Pacheco Grant. Don Bernardo de Miera y Pacheco was born on August 4, 1713, in Valle de Cariado, Cantabria, Spain. He married María Estefana Domínguez de Mendoza. Don Bernardo and his family

A view of Zuni Pueblo ancestral lands, now a part of the growing city of Rio Rancho. The city interconnects with lands of Santa Anna, Jemez and Sandia Pueblos. *Photo by Rosa María Calles, 2018.*

moved to Santa Fe from Chihuahua in New Spain. He is perhaps the most famous person during the Spanish colonial period of New Mexico history to petition for a land grant. Bernardo de Miera y Pacheco was a mapmaker who executed the earliest maps of New Mexico. He was an expert in knowing not only about the topography of the territory but also about how far each area extended. It is obvious that government officials consulted him when other grants of land were given. He was not only a noted cartographer but also an artist of religious images for the churches. He served as a captain of engineers for the Spanish Royal Corps of Engineers. His maps are recognized for their attention to detail as far as ethnography, geological formations and geography are concerned. The captain's maps were used for reference well into the Mexican period in dispensing land grants. In 1749, he mapped the Rio Grande River and its tributaries. In 1758, Governor Marín del Valle procured the services of Miera y Pacheco, who produced maps of the territory of New Mexico from June 1, 1757, until December 1757. He produced a highly detailed and illuminated map of New Mexico for del Valle. Don Bernardo served as a cartographer for the Domínguez-Escalante Expedition in 1776. He also accompanied the famed expedition of Governor Juan Bautista de Anza in 1779 into California. In 1803, American mapmaker Alexander von Humboldt used Miera y Pacheco's maps to prepare his own maps, which he in turn presented to U.S. president Thomas Jefferson. These maps helped to precipitate the Lewis and Clark Expedition and other American explorations into Spanish territory. Miera y Pacheco's own very significant explorations and maps, however, have not been credited in U.S. history.

On February 9, 1768, Governor Fermín de Mendinueta awarded an extensive grant of lands to Miera y Pacheco for his services, and also to Don Pedro Padilla. Francisco Trébol Navarro, the *alcalde* (mayor) of Alburquerque, was instructed by the governor to survey the land. Navarro found no legal obstacles to the land grant, so he issued a *testimonio*, or testimony, for the protection of the grantees on March 12, 1768. Extant records prove that this grant was indisputable. Bernardo and María Estefana had two sons, Anacleto and Manuel. Anacleto's daughter María de Miera y Pacheco married Flemish soldier Josef Gálvez. Their daughter María Gálvez married Andrés Calles, whose descendants would be inheritors of the Tome Land Grant. Captain Miera y Pacheco was also granted a land grant in the Cebolleta area. He held the office of alcalde of the villages of Galisteo and Pecos around 1758. He also served as godfather for several Pecos Pueblo Indians and Plains Indians who converted to Christianity. The

Surveyor General's Office on December 14, 1874, noted numerous Spanish colonial citations and documentations for confirmation of the Bernardo de Miera y Pacheco Grant. This grant was taken under advisement by the American government. In studying title to the Don Bernardo de Miera y Pacheco grant, the American government surmised:

> *The grantees were not vested with an absolute title to the land because it was not shown they had complied with the laws and regulations....It has been repeatedly held by the highest judicial tribunals of the country, both state and federal, that if anything remained to be done at the time of the acquisition of the territory from a foreign power, in order to vest a perfect title under the laws of such power, the title remained in the sovereign and passed to the United States.*

The government claimed there was no proof in existence that Miera y Pacheco and Pedro Padilla had ever occupied the land, even though the Surveyor General's Office on December 14, 1874, noted numerous Spanish colonial citations and documentations for confirmation of the Bernardo de Miera y Pacheco Grant. The American government insisted it should be rejected. It also quibbled with the original size of the grant, although the wording was quite specific, and attempted to contend that the area was considerably smaller, saying it covered just 4,428 acres, even though it would have originally been hundreds of thousands of acres.

On October 6, 1892, a Charles W. Lewis claimed he had purchased this grant from certain representatives of the heirs of Miera y Pacheco and Padilla. He sued for possession and official confirmation of the grant. On February 11, 1893, J. Akers claimed to be a lineal (possibly through marriage) heir and also filed suit for the property. An assignee of purported heirs also filed suit for the land. A U.S. court determined the genuineness of the original grant but argued it encompassed about 4,340 acres. Deputy Surveyor Albert F. Easley determined it was actually 4,106.66 acres, which was patented on March 6, 1911, to the new owners, Lewis and Akers, et al. It is not recorded if any of the descendants of the original grantees were ever recognized. The U.S. government claimed much of the area, as it also did in claiming the Ignacio Chávez Land Grant, which had been provided to Chávez in 1768. Means of absolute proof included paying taxes, as was done in the United States (U.S. property tax laws did not apply to Spanish and Mexican territories); documentary evidence deposited with the government at the capital city of Santa Fe (Spanish and Mexican citizens were not required to submit notarized statements of residency); and signed, sworn affidavits from nearby neighbors stating their knowledge of residency. The problem here was that the neighbors who lived miles away were also being required to submit these papers, and their residency was also being questioned.

During the Spanish colonial period in New Mexico, there were Spanish-born administrators who engaged in all governmental affairs. Some had been trained at the University of Salamanca as well as other places of higher learning in Spain. They were assigned to Santa Fe, in New Mexico, and some arrived with their families. Most left, but some stayed, such as the well-known Don Pedro Duran y Chávez family, including two sons, Fernando and Nicolás. This family is well known in New Mexico history, and the sons spawned hundreds of descendants, as did other families that arrived during the colonization of 1598. Therefore, in New Mexico, all descendants and heirs of the original settlers have a heartfelt stake in stolen lands. One such piece of land is situated in a community known as San Miguel.

A leading citizen of Santa Fe named Lorenzo Márquez went before Governor and Lieutenant Colonel Don Fernando Chacón in 1794, requesting land for himself, his family and other families. He pleaded that the capital city of Santa Fe was growing to the point that there was not enough farmland or pastureland for everyone. The city was rapidly expanding. The area simply could not accommodate growing local Spanish families, foreigners such as Frenchmen and other immigrants who were attempting to move in. He begged that more than fifty families needed land that they would all work hard on and cultivate, and that this would provide goods, revenues, livestock, fruit and vegetables for Santa Fe and the rest of New Mexico. After carefully considering the notable request, Governor Chacón granted what would be known as the San Miguel del Vado (Bado) Grant to Márquez and the families. The names of all of the men, women and children appeared on the community grant, and it was legally conveyed as required by Spanish law.

The grant was primarily situated along the *vados*, or banks, of the Pecos River thirty to forty miles from Santa Fe. Here, the settlers set up an irrigation systems called *acequias* (ditches), *acequia madre* (the mother ditch), *contracequias* (offshoots of the main ditch) and *renajes* (spillways of river water). The clear and continuous water from the mountains and springs fed lush pastureland, farmlands, vineyards, a multitude of fruit and vegetable trees and livelihoods for the inhabitants, such as weaving, wood furniture and sculpting and a variety of folk arts. San Miguel became a trading center on the Santa Fe Trail from Missouri to Santa Fe and a port of entry

Settlement and Sacrifice

Irrigation ditches (acequias) covered the fertile Rio Grande Valley. This provided rich farmlands for both Indians and Native Hispanics. *Photo by Ramón Juan Carlos de Aragón, 2001.*

for American merchants coming into the territory. At the port, merchants had to state their business, explain their purpose for entering, describe the merchandise they carried and pay a nominal fee to the government for trading. San Miguel also provided a buffer zone for warring nomadic Indian tribes such as the Comanches, Apaches and Navajos who continuously attacked and raided the Pecos Indian Pueblo. Warring tribes had done this for generations if not centuries. The Pecos Indians had managed to survive, but these attacks would spell the beginning of the end for them, despite protection by the Spanish military.

The San Miguel del Vado Grant spearheaded other approved grants of lands nearby for communities and individuals. Grants included the Los Trigos Grant, issued in 1814; the Alejandro Valle Grant of 1815; the Antonio Ortiz Grant of 1818, all issued under the Spanish government and the Luis Cabeza de Baca Grant of 1820, regranted as the Las Vegas Grant in 1835; the Antón Chico Grant of 1822; the Pino Grant of 1823; and the Tecolote Grant of 1824 given under the Mexican government. A Roman Catholic church was eventually built at the central village of San Miguel to serve more than one thousand inhabitants in what became a large plaza. The village then became an outlying administrative seat for the

A view of the Villanueva Valley. Parts of land grant sections now are the Villanueva State Park. *Ramón Juan Carlos de Aragón, 2001.*

government of Santa Fe. The jurisdictional area of San Miguel extended into northeastern New Mexico and the plains. This administrative seat had the authority to issue grants within its jurisdiction and monitor the correct use of these granted lands.

In 1751, Governor Tomas Vélez Cachupin issued the Las Trampas Grant as a community land grant because "it appears that the inhabitants of this city [Santa Fe] have increased to a great degree....There are lands which up to this point are uncultivated and which will yield rewards to those who cultivate them....The further benefit will result that hostile Indians will not go into them."

The Spanish government saw the settlement of these areas as protection of the capital city of Santa Fe. It would also add to the defense of Spanish frontiers. San Miguel became a military outpost, or presidio, replete with quarters for troops, stalls for horses and storage for needed supplies and armaments.

On March 12, 1803, Governor Cachupin ordered Don Pedro Bautista Pino to affirm that the lands of the San Miguel del Vado Grant were being lived on, cultivated and improved and that the descendants would inherit that interest in the common lands of the grant in perpetuity. He provided

Defensive rock walls at Villanueva. Citizen soldiers piled up rocks to protect the area from an invading Texan army in 1841. There was no protection from land thieves. *Photo by Ramón Juan Carlos de Aragón 2001.*

a glowing report and was also instrumental in dividing up parcels of lands. Don Pedro was equitable with his help with land distribution, keeping in mind that the San Miguel del Vado land did not interfere with the San José del Vado Grant upstream and the area belonging to Pecos Pueblo. He made an issue of the fact that the Apaches were killing the women and children of Pecos and that something needed to be done. Pino served as a delegate from New Mexico to the Spanish Royal Court from 1810 to 1813. While in Cádiz, Spain, Don Pedro Bautista Pino published a book with the title *Exposición Sucinta y Sencilla de la Provincia del Nuevo Mexico* (The short and succinct exposition of the province of New Mexico). This book was meant as a request to officials and the crown to provide more benefits for New Mexico and its citizens. Pino mentioned in the book: "During the administration of Governor Chacón, I was commissioned to...distribute lands to more than two hundred families. After I concluded this operation...my heart, at that moment as never before, was overcome with joy. Parents and little children surrounded me; all of them expressing, even to the point of tears, their gratitude to me for having given them land for their subsistence."

The year 1841 promised to be of great importance and great significance for San Miguel and its residents. An invasion force was approaching from the Republic of Texas. An army of more than two hundred men was bent on taking over New Mexico Territory. Texas hoped to take over the very lucrative trade on the Santa Fe Trail to help save the floundering republic. Conquering San Miguel would be the first step in the republic's plans. Next would be the capital at Santa Fe. Military intelligence flowed into San Miguel. A force from the village out on patrol spotted the movements of the approaching army. Governor and General Manuel Armijo immediately mobilized forces to augment those already at San Miguel del Vado. All able-bodied men with firearms from San Miguel were mustered into service. Several hundred made preparations.

Stone fortifications (still extant today at Villanueva State Park) were constructed near the village of Villanueva at San José del Vado. In short, the Texan army was soundly defeated and all of its soldiers were taken captive except for the deserters. Two soldiers from New Mexico received the equivalent of the Congressional Medal of Honor for their bravery and courage in the face of the enemy. One of them was Diego Archúleta, who later achieved the rank of colonel for his actions. After the Texan invasion of 1841, Colonel Archúleta conspired with American spy James Magoffin and received a purported substantial bribe for his treachery in personally disbanding New Mexico's troops in 1846, when the unsanctioned U.S. troops from Missouri invaded. Archúleta was promised a governorship for most of the territory by American officials. He never received the promised governorship, but he did receive a commission as a brigadier general in the U.S. Army for his collusion during the Mexican-American War.

In August 1846, Colonel Stephen Watts Kearny and his Missouri state troops arrived at Las Vegas, New Mexico, to presumably take over the territory in the name of the United States. He emphasized: "I now tell you that those who remain peaceably at home, attending to their crops and herds, shall be protected by me, in their property, their persons, and their religion; and not a pepper, not an onion, shall be disturbed or taken by my troops, without pay, or by consent of the owner."

Since the plaza of Nuestra Señora de Los Dolores de Las Vegas (Our Lady of Sorrows of the Meadows) was located in an area of farms and ranches, some located miles away, it can be easily surmised that very few residents heard Kearny's words. Locals were also used to his traveling with U.S. troops accompanying American wagon trains from Missouri to Santa Fe so he and his forces were not considered to be anything out of the ordinary. In addition, Kearny did not know Spanish, so he would have needed the services of an interpreter.

After Kearny and his force, including Mormon men, women and children arrived in Santa Fe, he immediately headed for California. There, he engaged Mexican lancers mounted on fleet horses, while he and his troops were mounted on mules. Mexican dragoons soundly defeated the Missouri force. Kearny, who had been promoted to brigadier general for his actions in New Mexico Territory, was badly wounded. The U.S. Congress eventually declared that the actions undertaken by Kearny and his officers were not officially sanctioned. These actions included the invasion of New Mexico and entering Mexican Territory. These were the roots of what was to come for New Mexico's land grants. After the United States took over New Mexico, the San Miguel del Vado Grant, dating from 1794, was confirmed at 315,000 acres. Don Faustina Baca y Ortiz petitioned the Surveyor General's Office for confirmation of the grant on March 18, 1857.

Mathew G. Reynolds, the U.S. attorney for the Court of Private Land Claims, wrote on June 26, 1894: "This case is important because of the fact that here is a large amount of these three hundred thousand acres that has never been used, or occupied beneficially by anybody, and any claim to which would not have been recognized by either the Spanish or Mexican governments, and should not be by our government."

The United States conveniently latched on to Reynolds's determination, although both the Spanish and Mexican governments had sanctioned and approved the grant along with its common lands for many generations. The Supreme Court immediately reversed the original decision of the Court of Private Land Claims prior to Reynolds and approved only 5,000 acres. A patent for 5,000 acres was issued in 1910. Land speculators, political officials and the U.S. government would claim 310,000 acres. The Court of Private Land Claims had been organized in Denver, Colorado, in July 1891. The office was later moved to Santa Fe, New Mexico. The following are examples of land grants confirmed by the Court of Private Land Claims: Juan Bautista Valdez Land Grant claimed 58,531.43 acres as a community land grant, and 1,468.57 acres were confirmed; Ojo Caliente Land Grant claimed 42,042.21 acres, with 2,244.98 acres confirmed as a community land grant and Cieneguilla Land Grant confirmed for 3,202.79 as an individual land grant; Santo Domingo Indian Pueblo and San Felipe Indian Pueblo Land Grants claimed 38,929.31 acres, and 1,070.688 acres were confirmed as ancestral Indian lands; and San Antonio de la Huerta Land Grant was confirmed for 4,763.85 acres as a community land grant out of 125,236.15 total acres.

2
SEEDS OF LAND STRUGGLES

I have no doubt many injustices occurred in stolen land grants. You have to look at the young people of today. They're the ones you've got to give some hope to.
—*Governor David F. Cargo, 1969.*

On March 16, 1848, the U.S. Senate ratified the Treaty of Guadalupe Hidalgo, ending the Mexican-American War. Article 10 was stricken by the U.S. government. This article was eliminated because the U.S. government was required to honor and guarantee all land rights that had been awarded to citizens by both the Spanish and Mexican governments to lands that were ceded to the United States when the treaty was signed. This essentially paved the way for taking New Mexico lands by both the government and private individuals wanting to capitalize on land opportunities. Dr. Myra Ellen Jenkins, director of the New Mexico State Records and Archives Center and a state historian, once said: "Approximately two hundred partially fraudulent or illegal claims perpetrated by various individuals took place in New Mexico after the United States took over....Tijerina has done what many thoughtful New Mexicans, myself included, had long hoped he would do, turn his organizing abilities, his charisma and his deep convictions toward peaceful methods of securing justice."

William A. Keleher (1886–1972), famed New Mexico attorney and author of *The Fabulous Frontier: Turmoil in New Mexico, Violence in Lincoln County, and the Maxwell Land Grant*, presented a paper at a joint meeting of the New Mexico

Bar Association and the Texas Bar Association in Amarillo, Texas, on July 5, 1929. In this paper, Keleher wrote:

> *The laws of Spain attempted to do justice to Indians in land matters; and as late as September 1, 1867, Benito Juarez, president of Mexico, issued a decree designed to protect the Indians in their rights of ownership in land.... The rights of the Indians to the lands they actually occupy, and their rights to additional lands, have been the subject of endless litigation, and investigation by Congress.... Land grant litigation in New Mexico has concerned itself with treaties; with documents purporting to support titles to grants; with conditions annexed to grants; with questions of inheritance; with the law of evidence as to boundaries; with the rule as to proof of foreign laws, usage and customs; with ejectment, partition, statutes of limitation; with the powers of the congress of the United States; and the powers of courts of private land claims and other related legal questions... in connection with claims made before the Court of Private Land Claims in New Mexico, established by Act of Congress on March 3, 1891.... The Court of Private Land Claims heard 301 petitions, involving 34,653,340 acres of land, finishing its work June 30, 1904.... There were many suits in the district courts, and a number of them were appealed to the supreme court. Some of the suits, because of the small value of the land, inability of heirs to finance litigation, vexatious legal questions, and discouraged and disheartened counsel, were abandoned. As a result, there are today in New Mexico some parcels of land, unclaimed, to all practical purposes, and known as "lost land grants."... The lost land grant in New Mexico has a counterpart in ghost land grants, of which the so-called Rayuela and Beales Grant is an interesting example. The title to all farming lands in Quay County, New Mexico, is overshadowed by this ghostly grant, which has haunted abstracters, lawyers and loan companies in that particular county since November 17, 1916. On that date there were filed a number of instruments purporting to convey title to practically all of the public domain in Quay County, among them being a purported certified copy of a petition signed by José Manuel Rayuela, asking the establishment of a land grant; and warranty deeds in a chain of title purporting to convey approximately one million acres of land. Apparently there never was a grant...this so-called grant was litigated in the case of Interstate Land Company V. Maxwell Land Grant Co., 41 Fed. 275, and on appeal to the supreme court of the United States as reported in 139 U.S. 569.... The lands claimed to have been granted to Rayuela and Beales became public domain*

Maxwell Land Grant.

FARMING LANDS UNDER IRRIGATION SYSTEM.

These farming lands with perpetual water rights are now being offered for sale in tracts of forty acres and upwards. Price of land with perpetual water rights from $17 to $35 per acre, according to location. Payments may be made in ten year installments. Alfalfa, Grains, Fruits of all kinds, and Sugar Beets grow to perfection

GOLD MINES.

On this Grant, about forty miles west of Springer, New Mexico, are the gold mining districts of Elizabethtown and Baldy, where important mineral discoveries have lately been made. Claims on unlocated ground may be made under the Mining Regulations of the Company, which are favorable to the prospector as the U. S. Government Laws

Near Raton, New Mexico, on this Grant, are located the COAL MINES of the Raton Coal and Coke Company, where employment may be found at good wages for any wishing to work during the seasons that farming or prospecting can not be successfully done.

For particulars and advertising matter apply to

THE MAXWELL LAND GRANT CO.
RATON, NEW MEXICO

Dubious land grant companies sprang up overnight attempting to capitalize on easy money taken from gullible people willing to steal lands from rightful owners. *Author's collection.*

of the United States and thousands of acres have been homesteaded.... However, the ghost of this particular grant still haunts the land, because as late as a few months ago an unsuccessful effort was made to have the New York Title and Mortgage Co. issue a policy of title insurance on the so-called Beales property for one million dollars.

The endless struggle to regain lost land grants is one that has adversely affected many communities in New Mexico. It is asked, why do tears still run down the swollen eyes and cheeks of saddened Hispanic people in the towns and villages of New Mexico? It is because they lost lands paid for by many sacrifices of their venerable ancestors. These sacrifices included loss of life, pain and suffering and the daily struggles of farming and ranching.

They worked from sunup to sundown. Loved ones were buried on these lands. The members of those families living on these timeworn lands were called Penitentes. Both men and women dedicated their lives to the passion sufferings of Jesus Christ and his most sorrowful mother, Mary. During the most holy season of Lent, passion plays produced throughout New Mexico continued a tradition that was centuries old. San Isidro, the venerated saint of farming, was prayed to for bountiful crops. Other saints, portrayed as carved wooden statues in the round and painted on wood panels, performed miracles that served those who worked and gave up their lives for their sons' and daughters' futures.

The struggle for lands is immemorial. Ancient peoples fought often for control of pieces of land. This is as old as humanity. Lives were lost and people were maimed as Vikings spread control of their power. Before this, the Romans and Carthaginians, as well as the Egyptians, sought to spread their borders. The Muslims wanted to take over the known world with a "Jihad," a holy war geared for control of the known world. Native Americans throughout the Western Hemisphere from North to South America fought constantly for control of lands and the spread of their empires. Captured victims were sacrificed to gods in hopes of divine support in the taking of lands and peoples.

Farming and grazing lands in northern New Mexico drew American cattle breeders and monopolists trying to capitalize on stealing the lands. *Photo by Ramón Juan Carlos de Aragón, 2001.*

After the English colonies won their freedom in the eastern United States, the new American government set its sights on expanding its territory to control Native American lands, as well as lands that had been owned by Spanish colonists and settlers for generations. In the East, the dominance of Englishmen over Native American rights and centuries-old control of lands was intentionally overlooked. As to incursions into Spanish settlements, the excuse was used that the Spanish abused Native American rights; therefore, land and water rights could be appropriated, taken over by American homesteaders and opportunists. Herein lies the roots of the abuse suffered by Hispanic and Indian residents in the Southwest in general and in New Mexico in particular.

RINGS OF LAND THIEVES

In the Spanish territories, which included the present-day U.S. states of California, Arizona, Texas, Nevada, Florida and New Mexico, there was a system of land partitions called Las Mercedes (land grants). The Spanish government as well as governors awarded lands to individuals, families and communities. Those willing to settle the lands and improve them could pass the lands on to their families. Millions of acres were provided for communities and colonization. These early pioneers dug irrigation ditches, channeling water from rivers to vast farmlands and these channels spread over countless acres. Much of this irrigation system still exists today, providing water for farming. Common lands owned by all and inherited by the grantees were used for grazing livestock, woodcutting and hunting. Spanish representatives also sought to protect and honor the lands of the Indian tribes.

In *Overview of Land Grants in New Mexico* (no date, published by the New Mexico Office of the State Historian), it is stated:

> *The United States government began its occupation of New Mexico in 1846. The Treaty of Guadalupe-Hidalgo established New Mexico as part of the United States in 1848. The treaty stated that, "property of every kind now belonging to Mexicans not established there shall be inviolably respected." To validate these land claims the United States government established the office of the Surveyor General. The mission of this office was to determine "the origin, nature, character, and extent to all claims to lands under the laws, usages, and customs of Spain and Mexico." In*

New Mexico's Stolen Lands

1891, the United States government established the Court of Private Land Claims to adjudicate land claims in New Mexico and other states because the Office of the Surveyor General was not successful in confirming the validity of New Mexican land grants.

One example of unethical practices by the Office of the Surveyor General was the Antón Chico Land Grant, which was petitioned by Manuel Rivera and twenty-two men in 1822. The grant "was clearly a community grant under Mexican law. At the time of confirmation of the grant under United States law, Surveyor General Henry Atkinson attempted to change the status of the grant to a private grant and deed it to the New Mexico Land and Livestock Co., of which he was president. This legal maneuver failed in the courts, but illustrates the level of corruption that prevailed in the Surveyor General's office."

A story carried by the *New York Times* in its May 18, 1884 issue with the title "New Mexico's Land Ring: Gigantic Swindles Accomplished in the Territory" brought the land theft issue to the national forefront. In New Mexico, Santa Fe Ring members pretty much ignored the issue and continued unabated in their goal of taking over land, mines, minerals, and water. In 1885, when the New Mexico Bureau of Immigration was in full swing, President Grover Cleveland appointed Edmund G. Ross governor of the territory. The new governor's claim to fame was having cast the deciding vote saving President Andrew Johnson from impeachment during Ross's tenure as a U.S. senator from Kansas. Governor Ross, on taking office, wrote, "It is notorious that possession of large quantities of the public lands has been obtained under the form of preemption laws through the boldest perjury, forgery and false pretense, and that in some instances, this has been done, if not with the connivance, at least through the inadvertence and the carelessness of public officials."

Of special note is that Governor Ross was featured in the 1956 Pulitzer Prize–winning book *Profiles in Courage*, coauthored by U.S. senator John F. Kennedy, who later became president. On May 11, 1885, President Cleveland appointed George W. Julian surveyor general of New Mexico. Julian was asked to "co-operate with the president in breaking the 'rings' of that territory." According to Julian, the president considered the investigation into land theft to be of the utmost importance. The new surveyor general started his official duties on July 22, 1885. After his investigations were completed, Julian submitted his findings to the president and published them in an article, "Land-Stealing in New

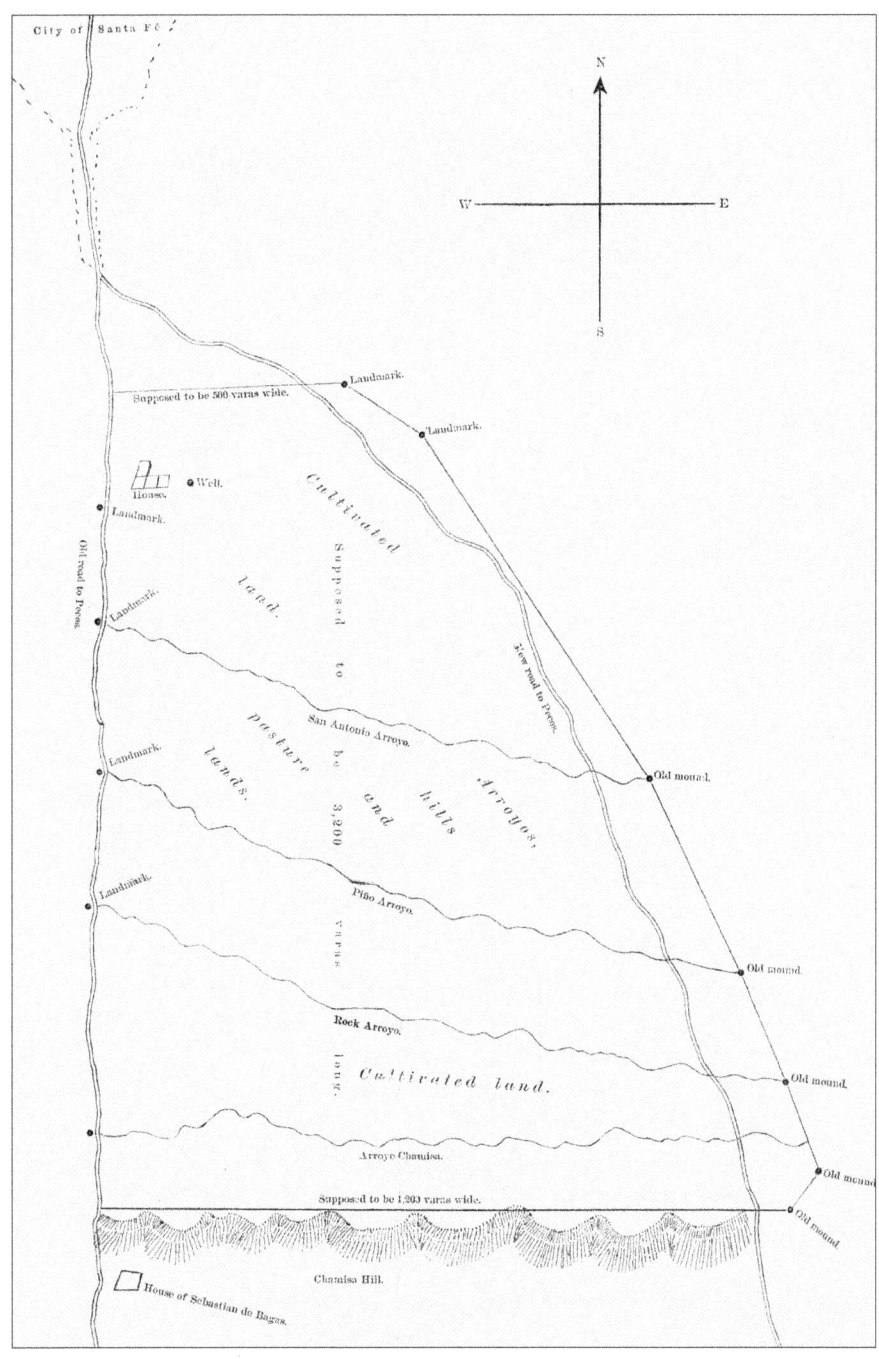

No training was needed for U.S. surveyors. A mule or a horse and willing to travel to remote areas was needed. Surveys were poorly done. *Author's collection.*

Americans try crossing the Rio Puerco in search of land opportunities. In time, Americans attempted to claim all lands even if they were arid. *Unknown photographer, c. 1929. Author's collection.*

Mexico," in the *North American Review* (145, no. 368 [July–December 1887]). Julian wrote:

> *In dealing with this subject I shall confine myself in the present article to the single topic of Spanish and Mexican land grants. When New Mexico was ceded to the United States the estimated area of these grants was about twenty-four thousand square miles, or a little over fifteen million acres.... The Treaty of Guadalupe Hidalgo of 1848, and the Law of Nations, obliged the United States to respect the title of all of these grants, so far as found valid under the laws of Spain and Mexico; and to this end the Act of Congress of July 22, 1854, was passed, creating the office of Surveyor-General for the Territory, and making it his duty to "ascertain the origin, nature, character, and extent" of these claims.*

Following Surveyor General Julian's tenure and investigation in New Mexico, the overall land situation got steadily worse. An editorial titled "Most Favorable Time" in the *Albuquerque Journal-Democrat* of August 6, 1899, stated the following:

> *To make matters worse, the real grants, numerous enough certainly, were largely out-numbered by fraudulent and spurious claims, which grew up under manipulation of keen and unprincipled speculators, who sought the country shortly after its acquisition from Mexico.... One illustration will*

> *suffice. It is the famous Peralta-Reavis claim, which covered 12,500,000 acres, and was supported by forgeries of decrees of judgment, grants and writs of judicial possession, while copies of the forgeries were filed in the archives of Arizona, New Mexico, and California, and various places in Mexico and Spain. Even church records were changed to show marriages, births and deaths of people who never existed, but an account of who was necessary to create chain of title. It is estimated that the claimant collected more than a half million dollars from various parties and interests, for privileges upon this grant, and yet the claim was fraudulent in toto.....No one would buy from the grant claimants, because pending determination of title the lands were withdrawn from settlement. Finally, the court of Private Land Claims was authorized by congress, appointed by the president and began work in 1893. It found it self confronted by something like 275 cases, aggregating in claimed areas about 50,000,000. In addition, seven suits, which were dismissed for palpable spuriousness on the very face of the papers, claimed 3,000 square leagues. It need scarcely be said that these grants, true and false, covered much of the best portions of New Mexico and Arizona....In the six years the court has been engaged upon these grants, it has disposed of about 30,000,000 acres, confirming to the claimants some 3,000,000 or more acres, and restoring the remainder to the public domain. In either case, these 30,000,000 acres, in round numbers, which before were not possible to purchase, are now open to the public, about nine-tenths being government land. This is why New Mexico just now holds such wonderful inducements to immigrants.*

The manipulation of land fraud was taking place on many fronts, executed by U.S. government officials, private merchants and politicians. Spanish documents were often simply composed by hand, so they were easily altered by unscrupulous individuals to lay foundations for claims and chains of title to lands. The most notorious case, which gained national and international attention, was the land theft perpetrated by the notorious James Addison Reavis. Because of tight political connections, U.S. senators Thomas B. Catron and Thomas Dorsey, as well as other members of the infamous Santa Fe Ring who included wealthy, and successful merchants, powerful attorneys, land speculators and former officers, and soldiers of the Confederacy, were involved in stealing lands in New Mexico. In addition, former Confederates were bent on seeking revenge in New Mexico for their loss in the Civil War.

James Addison Reavis, a former Confederate States of America soldier, was born on May 10, 1843, in Henry County, Missouri. He and his family eventually moved to Montevallo, Missouri. Reavis enlisted in Hunter's Regiment of the Confederate army. As a soldier, he practiced forging Confederate orders and passes, allowing him to move around at will. He even sold fraudulent passes to other Confederate soldiers to earn extra money. When his superiors were about to have him arrested, Reavis forged his own discharge papers, crossed military lines and surrendered to Union forces, thus escaping prosecution. He temporarily joined the Union until the war ended.

After the Civil War, James Reavis became a real estate agent. Reavis was proficient in altering real estate paperwork and forging property titles for those who paid him for his services. He aided those who did not have clear titles to lands and supported dubious land transactions. He became adept at finding faded eighteenth-century American parchment documents that could be cleaned of ink, and he reproduced titles with aged inks. Reavis met snake-oil peddler George M. Willing Jr. some time in 1871. Willing convinced Reavis that he had purchased an ancient Spanish land grant from a Don Miguel de Peralta in New Mexico for $20,000 in gold dust. Apparently, Willing was very convincing, and he made a transfer of rights to supposed lands to Reavis and others. Willing tried to sell fraudulent mining interests to a James D. Monahan in Prescott, Arizona. But Monahan grew suspicious and quickly left town.

Bogus Claims

After the American takeover of New Mexico Territory that included present-day Arizona, parts of Colorado and other vast areas, including Indian Territory, land speculators flooded the region. The Apache and Navajo Indians were displaced from their lands, so Americans found a great opportunity to present bogus claims to government officials. Reavis had determined that the floodgates of prosperity were also opened for him when he met George Willing.

Willing joined a U.S. surveying team headed for Santa Fe, New Mexico. He quickly learned the ropes when he joined forces with Missouri lawyer William W. Gitt, who claimed to be an expert in Spanish land grants. Unknown to Willing, Gitt had a warrant out for his arrest in Mexico for a dubious land claim. Reavis was enthralled with what Willing and Gitt had put together concerning a supposed Peralta Land Grant, supposedly attested to by none other than former Mexican president Antonio López de Santa Anna. This grant of land would spread in all directions, including parts of Arizona and New Mexico Territories, encompassing hundreds of thousands of acres.

George Willing died under mysterious circumstances, so Reavis found himself pretty much alone in claiming ownership of the Peralta Grant. In his now personal scheme, James Reavis learned about the U.S. Government Land Commission. The commission had confirmed or denied numerous land claims; it confirmed fraudulent claims if the person filing paid for the expenses incurred by the commission agents while on the job, since the government provided pecuniary funding for the operations of this office. A common practice of this agency was the acceptance of bribes, paid to officials for the confirmation of frivolous grants in New Mexico, Arizona, California and, most likely, Colorado and Texas as well.

After coming into possession of Willing's forged papers on the Peralta Grant, Reavis began to follow through on the transfers to him. He laid a claim to the present-day cities of Globe, Phoenix, Tempe, Florence and Casa Grande, Arizona, and lands that stretched into New Mexico. All of this area at the time was in New Mexico Territory. Curiously, in Reavis's forged documents from the King of Spain to a fictional baron of Arizona, Don Miguel Nemesio Silva de Peralta de la Córdoba deeded to Don José Gastón Silva y Carrillo de Peralta de las Falces de Mendoza and his wife, Doña Francisca María de la Córdoba y Muñiz Pérez, thousands of acres in 1708. Among the surnames was the Spanish word *falces*, meaning "sickles" or "scythes." Reavis was indeed using a scythe to cut through the legality of thousands upon thousands of land grant acres.

According to the Reavis documents, Don Miguel lived to be 116 years old. Reavis wrote anonymous reports he sent to newspapers, wherein he stated that there was irrefutable evidence that fully substantiated both the history of the Peralta Land Grant and the chains of title to him. He learned some Spanish and began calling himself Jaime Rivas. Other Americans entering New Mexico did the same, including Tom Catron, who called himself Tomas Catron, and a Jewish merchant named Louis Gold, who called himself Luis Oro. The name of Louis Gold, alias Luis, appears in several New Mexico land grant claims that were confirmed to him.

The Southern Pacific Railroad had to lay tracks through the supposed Peralta Land Grant. James Reavis sold easements to railroad officials for

New Mexico's Stolen Lands

Santa Fe Trail wagon and railroad tracks side by side at Romeroville near Las Vegas, New Mexico. American immigrants seeking land flooded the territory. *Photo by James Furlong c. 1879.*

$50,000, a vast amount of money for the period. He was well on his way to becoming immensely wealthy. The Reavis collection of fraudulent documents wound up filling two trunks. Reavis succeeded in entering forged documents into archives in Spain and Mexico. Ascertaining some made-up documents would take experts in document research and history countless hours. Reavis filed Spanish cedulas, codicils, proclamations and wills, as well as witness accounts, to shore up his claims. He also claimed he was the owner of the eighteenth-century Hacienda de Peralta, which he rebuilt on the original foundations of the ruins near Casa Grande, Arizona. James Reavis sold a fraudulent mining claim for $25,000. His ruse was gaining ground rapidly.

Due to his complex history of conveyances, James Reavis found himself entangled in a series of difficulties with officials who questioned not only the claims but also the ongoing paper trail. His next order of business was to find a wife. He would claim that she was an heiress and the rightful descendant of old Don Miguel. He found a house servant in California to whom he promised riches beyond her wildest imagination if she would consent to support his claims. She agreed. While Reavis introduced his wife, Sophia, to luminaries in Spain and Europe, his claims experienced support back home in the United States from senators and congressmen. Only cursory inspections of Reavis's documents followed this.

Now the "Land Baron" began going by the name James Addison Peralta-Reavis. He filed claims on behalf of his wife, now renamed Doña Sophia Micaela Maso Reavis y Peralta de la Córdoba, the third baroness of Arizona. Reavis said his wife followed in descent from other barons established by orders of Spanish kings. Although the Reavis history was outlandish, James Reavis succeeded in fooling many gullible individuals. He went as far as to build a statue and monument to the nonexistent Don Miguel de Peralta in Mexico to further secure his fraud. In time, he set up a dummy land corporation called the Casa Grande Improvement Company to sell shares, offering investment opportunities to develop lands as prescribed by the U.S. government for the purpose of providing railroad easements, building roads and dams, placing telegraph lines and constructing irrigation canals. In the meantime, Reavis planned to sell water rights and livestock illegally appropriated on his supposed lands. He built barbed-wire fences and placed no trespassing signs on people's private properties and lands. His ideas caught on in New Mexico with other land opportunists. They also wrote up dubious documents and set up land and ranching companies to steal cattle and horses from individual Spanish American residents and communities.

At the height of his career, James Reavis purchased lavish residences in St. Louis, San Francisco and New York City. He and his wife dressed in the finest clothing, she resplendent in expensive jewelry and he in the finest tailored suits. The Reavis couple was so believable, with their wealthy dress styles and bearing, that they were considered royalty in Mexico and Spain. They entertained very wealthy donors who could support Reavis's many enterprises. His affluent, opulent and lavish lifestyle impressed both politicians and celebrities, whom he paid well to entertain his guests. Meanwhile, Hispanic ranchers and farmers who actually owned the lands in question rose up strenuously, but their complaints always fell on deaf ears. Newspapers took notice and pressed those in power to investigate.

When President Benjamin Harrison was inaugurated in 1888, he appointed Royal Johnson as surveyor general. After taking office, Johnson continued to investigate the Peralta Land Grant, work he had commenced years before. He finally completed his study with the help of others and released the "Adverse Report of the Surveyor General of Arizona, Royal A. Johnson, upon the alleged Peralta Grant: a complete expose of its fraudulent character." Johnson was praised as a hero in Arizona and the rest of New

A peaceful valley, which could be fenced up and owned. This was an unavoidable draw to American land speculators. An excuse they often gave was that they did not know the identities of the owners. *Photo by Rosa María Calles, 2018.*

Mexico Territory. Surveyor General Johnson's surprising discoveries of Missourian Reavis's documents included numerous incorrect Spanish word spellings and poor sentence structures, which did not correspond with existing documents of the various colonial periods held in Mexican and Spanish archives in Mexico City, Madrid and Santa Fe. Nor was there any supporting documentation in Spanish colonial records about the existence of a Peralta Land Grant.

Altered Documents

The most glaring discrepancies were the use of late nineteenth-century steel pens on what were supposed to be eighteenth- and early nineteenth-century documents of sheepskin and parchment. Quill pens, germane to those periods, and print styles were not found on the James Reavis documents. Seventeenth- and eighteenth-century documents have a very distinctive flowing *s* letter that resembles a long *f*. The present-day *s* developed gradually in use before and close to the middle of the nineteenth century. Therefore, papers and books can be dated even if dates are not written or printed on them.

On February 20, 1890, Lewis Goff, the commissioner of the land office, instructed Johnson to allow James Reavis time to file an appeal to the secretary of the interior in Washington, D.C. Reavis obtained the services of attorneys and filed a lawsuit against the U.S. Court of Claims. He sought $11 million in damages, claiming that the government had illegally appropriated lands and water rights owned by Reavis and his wife. In March 1891, the U.S. Court of Private Land Claims was created to establish and confirm land grants in previously held Spanish/Mexican and French territories. Reavis rushed to obtain witness depositions to confirm his wife's history and inheritance of the Peralta Land Grant. He succeeded in creating a substantial story, including details about his wife's life from 1879 to 1882.

U.S. congressman James Broadhead determined that the Peralta Land Grant history was legitimate. The government appointed a special attorney, Mathew Given Reynolds, who secured experts in the analysis of documents to assist him. Arriving back in Santa Fe, New Mexico, on his return from Mexico, having searched ancient documents, Sevaro Mallet-Prevost, an expert on Spanish and Mexican law and documents, became convinced that the history and lineage of a fabled Peralta Land Grant was completely false. Further investigations unraveled the complex history of James Reavis's purported Peralta Land Grant.

Many officials of the Mexican and Spanish governments determined that documents dealing with the Peralta Land Grant were not genuine. Several of James Reavis's attorneys withdrew from his cases, as he was low on funds and could not pay them. Things were now turning against him, and both politicians and very rich and influential citizens left him.

When the Peralta Land Grant Claim finally reached the courts, it was obvious that Spanish words used in the documents were nonexistent in the Spanish documents, such as *tentación* (temptation). *Falces*, used in one document as part of Sophia's surname, meaning "sickles," "scythes" or "short broadsword." Such clues were used to determine that the documents were indeed forgeries. A made up word used was *descrubudo* rather than *descrito*, the latter always found in Spanish and Mexican documents. Erasures and later entries were found on many documents. Multiple inconsistencies finally proved that James Reavis had perpetrated one of the most detailed and picture-perfect land frauds in Spanish and later Mexican territories until he was finally caught and brought to justice.

James Reavis, aka James Peralta Reavis, aka Jaime Peralta Rivas, as he became known among Hispanic residents, was finally arrested and charged with crimes. The criminal trial started on June 27, 1896. Witnesses who had been paid to corroborate Reavis's chains of title confessed to perjury. The prosecuting attorneys secured them to testify against Reavis. He was charged with forty-two counts of attempting to defraud the U.S. government. Of course, it was not brought up that Reavis was trying to displace a very large number of residents who had legitimate claims to the lands in question. Reavis was found guilty, fined $5,000 and sentenced to two years in prison. His sentence was reduced for good behavior.

After Reavis was released from prison, he once again attempted to get new investors for his development schemes. He completely ignored his previous sentence and continued to file land claims. This time, his grand visions fell on deaf ears, and he died penniless in Denver, Colorado, on November 20, 1914, although he had acquired millions through land fraud. A motion picture produced in 1950 called *The Baron of Arizona* starring Vincent Price featured a somewhat fictionalized version of the life of con man James Reavis and his fantastic ruse. An American rancher who had purchased Reavis Ranch land with horses and cattle got to keep the livestock as compensation from the courts for his loss. He changed the "PR" Peralta Reavis brand to "SB," for the Swindle Bar brand.

OTHER SWINDLES

The "wonderful inducements to immigrants" to migrate from Europe and the United States to New Mexico was the supposed widespread availability of land. This, of course, involved the massive takeover of grant lands. Another example of land grant corruption is the Cañon de Chama Land Grant, which was granted to Francisco Salazar, his brothers and twenty-eight other needy citizens in the Abiquiú area. Francisco Salazar wrote the request, naming the citizens who were requesting to build their town of San Joaquín in the center of the land grant. Alcalde Manuel Garcia de la Mora reported on July 14, 1806, "The section of the country is a very desirable one…and there is assigned them on the north and on the south one league for pastures, for on these two sides no injury can result, as there is neither a settlement nor a grant now made…and the said Cañon is distant from Abiquiú about five leagues."

By 1886, some of the Cañon de Chama Land Grant owners had left the original village of San Joaquín due to events that had taken place in New Mexico Territory. For example, a revolt against Mexico took place in 1837. A short-lived republic for all intents and purposes was proclaimed. There were continuous raids by marauding Apache, Comanche and Navajo Indians against the Spanish/Mexican towns and villages and the Pueblo Indian villages throughout New Mexico. Then the American Civil War disrupted the lives of the people with a Confederate invasion. Understandably, those who lived in isolated areas moved into larger towns for military protection. This was fodder for George W. Julian, an investigator for the government.

The highly controversial surveyor general got to work. For one thing, Old Spanish colonial documents were hard to read. Investigator Julian, as well as other Americans, could not read or write in Spanish. The flowery documents also contained abbreviations for words that couldn't be understood or were hard to interpret. Although descendants of the original Spanish colonists returned to their homes, ranches and farms in more peaceful times, Julian conveniently proclaimed those lands abandoned and should be taken over by the federal government without consideration of events that had taken place or were taking place. This was a flagrant violation of the Treaty of Guadalupe Hidalgo, which officially ended the Mexican-American War. Julian clashed with Thomas Benton Catron and the Santa Fe Ring because, sometimes, two claims interlocked over the same extensive areas. Julian felt that those unscrupulous American individuals, some of whom were former Confederates or Southern sympathizers and had connections in the U.S. Congress and Senate, were simply trying to claim lands that should indisputably belong to the U.S. government and the Union as a result of military conquest. Julian often proclaimed that "there was no delivery of possession," even when there was unquestionable documentary evidence and clear chains of title to the heirs of the Spanish/Mexican grants and descendants of the original grantees. When he did recommend confirmation from the U.S. Congress, it would most often be for extremely reduced acreage rather than the actual claimed acres of land granted to the Spanish/Mexican citizens or Native Americans.

EARTH HUNGER

According to J.J. Bowden, "Speculators and 'earth hungry monopolists' quietly began to purchase scores of outstanding interests under the Chama Grant....The new owners instituted suit in that forum for the confirmation of their title." In 1894, the Court of Private Land Claims deemed the grant valid but reduced it to 1,422 acres. In 1905, a patent was issued to Thomas D. Burns and the Rio Arriba Land and Cattle Company. The lands were

View of Sandia Mountains from Indian Pueblo lands. The city of Albuquerque and other cities of New Mexico annexed land grant lands and Indian lands as needed. *Photo by Rosa María Calles, 2018.*

never returned to the descendants of the original Cañon de Chama Land Grant owners. Thomas D. Burns removed all of the remaining families residing on the patented acres, which were later acquired by the federal government. Until 2013, the families of the area were also denied access to the community cemetery.

There are many examples of this type of action, which clearly went against the Treaty of Guadalupe Hidalgo. Another such example is the Bartolomé Baca Grant. Baca died in 1834. In 1845, the Mexican government granted Antonio Sandoval 415,000 acres for "his services to the government of Mexico." The property was within the boundaries of the land grant given to Baca in 1819. Baca's heirs never contested it until 1877, when Baca's grandchildren sold the grant to Manuel A. Otero. Sandoval sold the grant to Gervasio Nolan. Nolan's heirs sold their claim to the grant to Boston capitalist Joel Whitney. James Whitney, Joel's brother, with armed men took over Otero's ranch. The action ended with the death of Otero and other members of the household. James was arrested, but Joel helped him escape. James Whitney returned a year later and was charged with murdering Manuel Otero. He was taken to court and found not guilty by a corrupt court. James died from illness shortly after he was released. In 1901, the U.S. Supreme Court declared the Estancia Grant, formerly the Bartolomé Baca Grant, invalid. Both the Sandoval and Baca successors lost all claims to the land.

BROKEN LAWS

In 1836, José Julian Martínez and several families asked for lands to settle and colonize. Governor Albino Pérez approved the La Petaca Land Grant for 186,977 acres. The Office of the Surveyor General and the Court of Private Land Claims successfully reduced the total number of acres to 1,392. The U.S. Supreme Court ruled that international law was broken with a substantial reduction in the common lands that had been indisputably held by land grant heirs for generations.

In 1841, Francisco Aragón petitioned Governor Manuel Armijo for a grant of land. This became known as the Chillili Land Grant and was approved for 88,345 acres. As had been done before by the Spanish government and the Mexican government that followed, awards of grants were sometimes given as a reward to citizen settlers for previous military service. In this case, some grantees had distinguished themselves in conflict with a Republic of Texas invasion force. The surveyor general recommended confirmation of 23,686 acres. This grant is located in Torrance and Bernalillo Counties. The grant was converted into an agricultural cooperative in 1943. All of the common lands belonging to the heirs were sold off by the cooperative without the approval or consent of the descendants of the original heirs.

Lorenzo Márquez and fifty-one individuals petitioned the San Miguel del Vado Land Grant in 1794. Governor Don Fernández Chacón approved the petition for 315,300 acres. Proceedings before the Office of the Surveyor General and the Court of Private Land Claims confirmed 5,147 acres. This land grant is located in San Miguel County. The grant was then finally confirmed for the original 315,300 acres. The U.S. government appealed the case to the U.S. Supreme Court, which forced the Court of Private Land Claims to reduce the acreage to around 5,000 acres.

Rapacity Galore

George W. Julian emphatically decried what he called "earth-hunger" in New Mexico. He arrived in the territory appalled by what he had heard about the outrages that were occurring. Of course, he had a preconceived notion that former Spanish and Mexican citizens were deeply involved in attempting to steal lands that rightfully belonged to the U.S. government by decree of conquest. He immediately set out to disprove any and all land grant claims. He also set his sights on the land-grab swindles practiced by Americans who had migrated to the territory. It made no difference to him that these individuals had busied themselves with also stealing lands from the native Mexican and Indian populations. An outraged Julian said:

> *It was inexcusable and shameful surrender to the rapacity of monopolists of 1,662,764 acres of the public domain, on which hundreds of poor men* [Americans] *had settled in good faith, and made valuable improvements, while it is calamitous to New Mexico as it has been humiliating to the government. I have already referred to the Ortiz mine grant, in which congress was induced to unite with the Surveyor-General in squandering upon private parties over 69,000 acres of exceedingly valuable mineral*

land, which the Mexican government never granted...(Congress) has criminally surrendered to monopolists not less than 5,000,000 acres, which should have been reserved for the landless poor [Americans].

While referring to Thomas B. Catron and the Santa Fe Ring in his further outrage, Julian stated:

The influence of these claimants over fortunes of New Mexico is perfectly notorious. To a fearful extent they have dominated governors, judges, district attorneys, legislatures, surveyors general and their deputies, marshals, treasurers, county commissioners, and the controlling business interests of the people. They have confounded political distinctions and subordinated everything for the greed for land. The continuous and unchecked ascendency of one political party for a quarter of a century has wrought demoralization in the other. T.B. Catron is a leading Republican, and C.H. Gildersleave, an equally prominent Democrat, but no political nomenclature fits them. They are simply traffickers in land grants. And recognized captains of this controlling New Mexico Industry...the grinding oligarchy of land sharks, whose operations have so long been the blight and paralysis of the Territory, should be completely routed and overthrown.

Community ruins. Many homes and towns in New Mexico were abandoned when residents were forced out. They had to move into cities and look for work. *Photo by Rosa María Calles, 2009.*

Native Americans believed in the spirituality of water as a life-giving force to be protected and cherished. Americans regarded water as a commodity. *Photo by Rosa María Calles, 2016.*

Julian did not consider himself a land shark, but he was working under the direction of the president of the United States to use any means he could to declare Mexican lands as rightfully a part of the public domain. He did succeed, and the government essentially confiscated millions of acres of land grants for national forests, as well as leases for ranching conglomerates; oil drilling; gold, silver and copper mining; timber; water resources; and homesteading. Both Spanish/Mexican land grants and Indian lands became part of this stolen domain for the interests of the few; entire communities and families were forcefully removed through collusion and malfeasance.

CAT'S NAILS

Fern Lyon, in a 1984 issue of the periodical *La Gaceta* (IX, no. 1, El Corral De Santa Fe Westerners), was quoted from a paper she had presented at a meeting.

The Santa Fe Ring seemed to control most of the real estate in the Territory. Ring leaders were generally supposed to be the newly elected Territorial Delegate to congress, Stephen B. Elkins, and Territorial United States attorney, Thomas B. Catron....President Rutherford B. Hayes was forced to do something....What he did, of course, was send a man to make a study....The special investigator's name was Frank Warner Angel....Territorial Surveyor General Proudfit had been replaced by H.M. Atkinson....At a hearing before the new Surveyor General, a hearing that was a direct result of Angel's investigation, the Uña de Gato Grant had been declared a fraud by the Department of the Interior and it was affirmed as public land, open to homesteaders....A U.S. Senator from Arkansas, Stephen W. Dorsey, who had bought the Uña de Gato was busily building a big house [mansion] *at Mountain Spring in the middle of the grant. As a result of the hearings, he was able to hustle to try to save his property. His method was to have henchmen homestead the land of the grant, then he bought the homesteads—a standard land grabbing technique of the day.*

It is noted that in Colfax County records of deeds in books listed as "B," "C," "D" and "E," dating from 1878 to 1882, more than three hundred were listed as approved homesteads by the U.S. government and later transferred to Senator Dorsey, who is now acknowledged to have been a Santa Fe Ring member. Extensive areas of the purported grant included portions of the Las Vegas Land Grant, the Mora Land Grant and other grants of northern New Mexico. When the railroad system was being planned for New Mexico, American businessmen, politicians and attorneys, such as T.B. Catron, saw enormous possibilities to vastly enrich themselves. Therefore, a plan was put into operation to displace Spanish/Mexican citizens of their individual and community land grants and sell rights-of-way at tremendous profits to the railroad. Coal, minerals and metals that previously existed or were found on those lands were also sold invalidly. Timber on the lands was used for railroad ties and lumber for buildings. Individual property owners were forced out of their homes, and entire communities ceased to exist. Those who would not leave willingly were forced to vacate under threats to their lives. At times, people were tortured and even murdered. Fern Lyon continued, "Dorsey never did say who sold him the grant or how much he paid for it."

Lyon mentioned that a Lewis Kingman wrote a letter postmarked from Santa Fe on July 8, 1877, to one Henry Arms, stating:

I have taken considerable trouble to look into the matter from facts which I have ascertained I find that when the papers were first gotten up some time [in] *the latter part of '72, or early in '73, they were brought to John Gwin, Elias Brevoort, then to David J. Miller of the Surveyor Gen's office to examine the original papers, the paper signed by Armijo* [this most probably was being passed off as a grant presumably issued by former Mexican governor Manuel Armijo] *is of blue tint with watered lines drawn about one inch apart from top to bottom, the sheet is fearfully scratched but principally in diagonal lines across the paper— the signature of Armijo does not correspond with any of his others...a self-evident fraud.... To add to the cheek of the whole thing, the same parties have the last few months got another fraudulent grant through in Colorado....I am to give what information I can and oppose any frauds of this kind that may come up.*

Extensive parts of this fraudulent grant became lands of the famous Bell Ranch, other American and English cattle ranches and lands owned by Lucien B. Maxwell and many others. These lands are still in contention.

Las Vegas, New Mexico merchant Margarito Romero and family camping at El Porvenir on the Mora Land Grant. The powerful Romero family fought land injustice. *Unknown photographer, circa 1897. Author's collection.*

Settlement and Sacrifice

Easy Land

An article appeared in the *Albuquerque Journal-Democrat*, on Sunday morning, August 6, 1899, titled "Advantages of Colonies." It attempted to draw outsiders such as Americans and others to New Mexico.

> *But where it can be so arranged, it is better for settlers in New Mexico to come in communities consisting of anywhere from 10 to 100 or more, of course having previously sent their representatives to see the country and arrange for purchase. Such communities can secure admirable locations of 1,000 to 10,000 acres, either of government land or from proprietors of land grants, the latter being on very easy terms. These tracts would consist partly of valley lands for irrigation and partly mesa lands for pasturage. The colonists could construct their own irrigation systems and at a mere nominal outlay, by doing the work themselves. Though bought in a body, the lands could be divided and held in severalty.... The irrigation laws of New Mexico are quite favorable. All rivers and streams in the territory are declared to be public acequias, and no building, footpath or other work of human hands must be allowed to obstruct the free flow of water for*

The railroad system moved into New Mexico Territory. Land thieves sold rights-of-way. Some railroad officials belonged to the Santa Fe Ring. Telegraph poles went up on Indian lands. *Author's collection.*

irrigation. All the inhabitants of New Mexico have the right to construct either public or private acequias, and to take their water supply wherever it can be obtained.

It is impossible to review the history of lost land grants and Indian lands in New Mexico and tell the story in detail. Each struggle would be its own book. The rise and fall of a people who settled and sacrificed for generations since 1598 simply cannot be contained in one volume. It can be determined, however, that with the existing conditions of the time there was not much that the original owners of the lands could do. Their hands were "legally" tied up by the American political system when the Unites States took over. Each land grant story would be a book in itself due to the struggles and hardships that New Mexico residents went through as they lost their lands, water rights and livelihoods. Poverty took over, and now New Mexico ranks at the top in homelessness, suicide and hunger among U.S. states. There was no way to change the outcome. Cries and tears from the people fall on deaf ears as this story continues.

3
SHADOWS OF THEFT

Hispanic New Mexicans in the territory of New Mexico whose lands culture, history, heritage and customs were to be honored and protected under the Treaty of Guadalupe Hidalgo signed between the United States and Mexico to officially end the Mexican-American War found themselves in a quandary. Not only were their horses and cattle being stolen, but they were also the subjects of abuse, loss of rights and even murder. Many still sought to proceed through the courts and to protect themselves and their lands through the legal system. One such person was Doña Bárbara Chávez de Sánchez, after whom the community of Los Chávez near Albuquerque, New Mexico, was named.

The following patent was issued by President Teddy Roosevelt and countersigned by F.M. McKean, his secretary. C.T. Branch recorded the patent in the Records of the General Land Office:

> *Whereas, in accordance with the provisions of the Act of Congress approved the third day of March one thousand eight hundred and ninety-one, entitled, "An act to establish a court of private land claims and to provide for the settlement of private land claims in certain states and territories" the claim of Nicolás Duran de Chávez has been duly established to private land grant situated in Township five and six North of Range one West and Township five and six North of Range one and two East of New Mexico Meridian in the County of Valencia, New Mexico, containing thirty nine thousand and eight hundred and thirty seven acres and sixty-seven hundredths of an*

acre according to the plat and survey of said claim approved by the Court of Private Land Claims May 29, 1895. Been more particularly bounded and described as follows, to Wit: On the North by an East and West line drawn through the northern side of the ruins of the house of the said Nicolás Duran de Chávez on the East; by the Rio Grande del Norte; on the south by the northern boundary of the Belen Land Grant and in the West by the Rio Puerco....The United States of America, In consideration of the premises, have given and granted, and by these do give and grant unto the said Nicolás Duran de Chávez, and to his heirs, the lands above described: TO HAVE AND TO HOLD the same together with the rights, privileges, immunities, appurtenances, of whatsoever nature thereunto belonging, unto the said Nicolás Duran de Chávez and to his heirs and assigns forever...and that the said grant is made subject to all the limitations and terms of said Act of Congress of March 8, 1891. With the proviso however that the title from the United States to the lands heretofore patented to Robert M. Stockton, Bárbara Chávez de Sánchez and Venceslao Baca shall remain valid, not withstanding this patent....Whereof, I, Theodore Roosevelt President of the United States of America, have caused these letters to be made patent,

Ruins of a building on the San Miguel del Vado Land Grant. This grant was vastly reduced before it was confirmed and patented by the U.S. government. *Photo by Ramón Juan Carlos de Aragón, 2002.*

and the seal of the General Land Office to be hereunto affixed…GIVEN under my hand, at the city of Washington, the eight-day of February, in the Year of our Lord one thousand nine hundred and seven, and of the Independence of the United States the one hundred and thirty first.

At first glance, this patent for the Nicolás Duran de Chávez Land Grant appeared to be incontestable. In response to President Roosevelt's patent, unknown persons obliterated the eighteenth-century ruins of the Nicolás Duran de Chávez hacienda at an unknown date. The Rio Grande del Norte and the Rio Puerco both changed courses. This severely complicated things when American land speculators and squatters contested boundaries. The territory of New Mexico not only experienced an onslaught of shady land speculators; a tremendous number of American families seeking a better way of life and opportunities swarmed into New Mexico. They went to New Mexico right after the American Civil War. Southerners whose homes had been burned and plantations destroyed, also fled to the southwest attempting to escape the wrath of the U.S. government. It didn't make a difference if they were encroaching on Hispanic or Indian Lands. They felt they were entitled, since Mexico had been beaten. "Those lands are ours."

II

DISENCHANTMENT IN NEW MEXICO

The statute of frauds was unknown to the civil laws which were in force at the time of the acquisition of the territory now known as New Mexico....Forgery and the fabrication of documents proved a fine art in connection with the claims made before the Court of Private Land Claims in New Mexico, established by act of Congress on March 3, 1891.
—*William A. Keleher*

4
A CONFEDERATE INVASION

"Quantrill Raiders Invade New Mexico." This could have been a newspaper headline carried across the country after the Civil War. The aftermath of the great American Civil War meant former Confederate officers and soldiers searched for prime territory to move into. New Mexico was a main target. Major Joseph C. Lea of Quantrill's Guerrilla Raiders, along with several of his troops, fled into New Mexico Territory. This ruthless group of Confederates who sacked the towns of Olathe and Lawrence, Kansas, were being hunted by both Union and Confederate troops for massacres they committed and for their rapacious history. Buildings were burned and residents were killed during the Civil War. Many women were raped, and this epoch is recognized as the most horrific in in Kansas's history. Quantrill's Raiders stole horses and cattle and took black slaves. Lea and his forces swept into New Mexico. He joined Tom Benton Catron, another notorious Confederate soldier. Catron, a distinguished Confederate after also escaping into New Mexico, became the acknowledged leader of a corrupt group of lawyers, judges, lawmen, politicians and land speculators in New Mexico called the Santa Fe Ring. Lieutenant Colonel Manuel Antonio Chávez and his New Mexico Union forces had defeated the Confederate army at Glorieta. This time, Southern sympathizers and former Confederate States of America leaders and veterans would victimize New Mexico territorial land and its residents.

Some New Mexico governors, senators and congressmen used political power and breach of oaths, plus improprieties in office, to suit themselves.

E. A. FISKE.   *H. L WARREN*

FISKE AND WARREN,
ATTORNEYS & COUNSELORS AT LAW
SANTA FE, NEW MEXICO.

Will practice in the Supreme and all District Courts in the Territory. Special attention given to corporation cases; also to Spanish and Mexican Grants and United States Mining and other land litigation before the courts and United States executive officers.

Before and after 1881, many Santa Fe, New Mexico attorneys proclaimed themselves as experts in Spanish and Mexican land grants. They also stated expertise in mining lands. *Author's collection.*

These ruthless men amassed considerable wealth with stolen lands and personal properties, including livestock, as well as horse theft. A *Smithsonian Magazine* article states that when English European settlers and later Americans spread through Indian territories, there were thirty-three million buffalo, or bison, roaming freely throughout the country. In time, there were only twenty-three left, preserved in a government reserve and near extinction. Robes and other uses of buffalo hides were to blame. In addition, sharpshooters traveling in front of trains flagrantly shot buffalos because they impeded the travel of the trains. William F. "Buffalo Bill" Cody gained a widespread reputation for killing more than two hundred thousand buffalo by himself. His famous Wild West Show featured Indian chief Sitting Bull, and mock cavalry and Indian "shoot 'em ups" were featured attractions. The government's policy of defeating the Native Americans also destroyed the food supply; as a result, buffalo were killed and left to rot. Forest areas were obliterated so that deer and other natural food sources would be eliminated. Water sources were purposely contaminated and polluted in some areas to force people out.

In northeastern New Mexico, opportunists believed that the area of the Las Vegas de Nuestra Señora de los Dolores Grant—more than 500,000 acres—contained the best grasslands for ranching in the territory. Monies for laying railroad tracks and rights-of-way had already been paid to investment consortiums that did not own the lands. Telegraph lines were being erected through grant lands and Indian lands without express authority of rightful owners. There was a long history of collective grazing and common use of watering areas for farm animals, as well as common use of wood fuel and coal and hunting and fishing areas. Now these places were being fenced off, and land grant heirs were prohibited from entering lands that were being taken over by the government and outside investors. The original Spanish names of villages and areas were replaced on maps, and soon new names appeared on an 1895 Rand McNally map: Watrous, Fulton Kroenigs, Sands, Shoemaker, Albert, Bell Ranch, Liberty, Springer, Eden, Maxwell City, Lyn, Blanchard, Bover, Connell, Beenham, Barney, Clapham, Folsom, Emory Gap and Gray's Mesa.

Squatters were appearing everywhere and building hovels, or quickly built structures, sometimes in isolated areas or near rivers, ponds and small lakes. Under U.S. law, squatters were allowed to use the land of another as long as the owner made no attempt to evict them. "Adverse possession" could eventually convert occupation of the property to title.

Ex-Confederate T.B. Catron served as a district attorney for the Third Judicial District Court in southern New Mexico, an area that included Lincoln, New Mexico. The famous Lincoln County War involved members of the Santa Fe Ring, cattleman John Chisum, William H. Bonney ("Billy the Kid"), famous sheriff Pat Garrett and many outlaws and gunmen. The "Law of the West" was the law of the gun. Land grant locals lost everything, including, in some cases, their very livelihoods and lives. "Big Boss" Catron was appointed attorney general for New Mexico. Later, President Ulysses S. Grant appointed him as a federal attorney. Catron's ambitions and corruption increased but with no justice applied to his and his cohorts' actions. Public and written complaints in the territory and in Washington mounted and became a thorn in the sides of members of the Ring. Could an assassination ploy work in their favor? On Saturday, February 7, 1891, the *Daily Citizen* in Albuquerque, New Mexico, contained a special report from the *Santa Fe New Mexican* about an attempted assassination at Santa Fe:

> *An attempt was last night made to assassinate Honorable Thomas B. Catron, member of legislative council from Santa Fe County. The murderous bullets, however, failed to reach their mark and the brunt of the cowardly act unfortunately fell upon Senator J.A. Ancheta of Grant County, five buckshot entering his neck and shoulders causing wounds.... The senators assembled last evening as was their wont, some sitting and others standing promiscuously about the large flat desk that occupies a place immediately in front of a glass door, and some six feet from the wall....Senator Mills sat near the right hand side from the window; nearly facing him, and on the opposite side of the desk, stood Mr. Catron, occasionally moving about the center of the room....Senator Stover sat on the left, at the foot of the desk and just out of range of the window so*

that he could scarcely be seen from the street. Senator Richardson was also there but excused himself and left. Mr. Gildersleeve had an appointment with the assembled senators but failed to keep it....Mr. Catron then sat down at the desk directly opposite Mr. Ancheta. About this time, 7:15 o'clock, Gus O'Brien, Mr. Catron's office-boy, who is also a page in the council, approached the office door and as he did so he saw a man leave the opposite side of the street and come across to a tree nearly opposite the office window....Mr. Catron was sitting in front of the window and plainly visible from the outside, the hurried footsteps of restive horses were heard in the street, and a second later two shots were fired, followed by the crashing of window glass....It is a deliberate attempt at assassination! Barney Spiers, of the Broad Guage saloon, saw the two horsemen who fired the shots. He was picking his way across the street from the plaza toward Mr. Catron's office going home....As they came past the window their horses were checked up for an instant and both fired. Then putting spurs to their horses the assassins dashed round the corner....The men went at breakneck speed up Palace avenue and turning southeast on Cathedral street, disappeared....In the group of senators, Mr. Catron was the central figure; the two assassins, it seems evident, took him for their target.

The *Daily Citizen* continued with regular reports on the condition of the patient and the illustrious career of the victim.

Latest from the Bedside of Senator Ancheta....Senator Ancheta is resting well improving, and out of danger. Judge Bail, his partner is here.... Paul Yrissari, of this city, and Senator Ancheta, who was shot Thursday night by cowardly Santa Fe assassins, attended school together at Notre Dame University, Indiana, years ago. While at college Mr. Ancheta was recognized as the brightest in his class, and when graduated he received the highest honors. As an orator he has few equals in the southwest.

Ancheta, nicknamed the "Golden Bull," was admitted in 1886 to practice law before the State of Indiana Supreme Court. He later moved to Santa Fe, New Mexico Territory, where he formed a partnership with John D. Bail in Santa Fe. Ancheta served as the district attorney for Grant and Sierra Counties. He maneuvered his way by 1891, four or five years after his arrival, into the ownership of the Mulato Mine, which he sold to the Haywood and Hobart Mining Company for $1,750,000. He sold the Pinos Altos Mine for

$141,000. He was a trusted member of Thomas Benton Catron's Santa Fe Ring. The newspaper story continued with Catron's interview:

> *Mr. Catron was called upon at noon and asked as to what he thought the motives of the assassins was. He replied that it undoubtedly had its origin in the condition of affairs that has existed in this county for the past two years. Interrogated as to whether or not he considered the assassin's blows as aimed at himself, he said he had no doubt but that it was, and could scarcely express surprise over it, as he had time and again, through friends, been warned that his life was in danger.*

The Power House in Santa Fe, which included Governor L. Bradford Prince, suspected that the militant group known as Gorras Blancas (white caps) was to blame for the shooting. Hispano natives in New Mexico, of course, saw this group of armed ranchers and farmers as freedom fighters seeking justice for themselves and their families. The American legal system had failed downtrodden people; it was known that governors, judges, lawyers and lawmen were bought and sold by powerful special interest groups. Minerals, precious metals and, eventually, natural resources such as oil, coal, lumber and water, among other things, were the source of internal court battles. At one point, Governor Prince and the Santa Fe Ring demanded the names of the night riders known as the Gorras Blancas who covered their faces to escape detection. Understandably, no one provided any information.

The legislature and governor at Santa Fe, New Mexico, continued with the prompt action on the attempted assassination with the posting of a reward on February 6 at a special council meeting, which took place at 10:00 a.m.

> *Mr. Catron introduced C.B. No. 122, an act making an appropriation for the arrest and conviction of persons concerned in the shooting and wounding of Hon. J.A. Ancheta, a member of the legislative council of the territory of New Mexico, was brutally and foully shot by some parties unknown, while in the discharge of his duties as a member of the judiciary committee of the council; and whereas, the said persons who attempted said assassination are now at large....That the governor of New Mexico be, and he is required and directed to offer a reward for the apprehension of the persons who shot and attempted to murder Hon. J.A. Ancheta on the evening of February 5, 1891, in the amount of $10,000* [$500.00 had been offered by Governor Lew Wallace for the apprehension of William H. Bonney ("Billy the Kid") in New Mexico; $5,000

was offered for the notorious Jesse James in the West], or $5,000 for each and every one of them, including any person implicated in or who instigated the same to be paid by any money in the treasury on the certificate of the governor and warrant of the auditor....A message announced that the house had passed joint resolution No. 7 offering a reward of $20,000 for the persons who shot and attempted to murder Hon. J.A. Ancheta on the evening of February 5, 1891.

GORRAS BLANCAS (NIGHT RIDERS)

On May 24, 1897, the U.S. Supreme Court ruled that common lands on community land grants not yet adjudicated belonged to the government. New Mexico territorial senators Stephen B. Elkins and Thomas Dorsey staked their claims. The 315,300.80-acre San Miguel del Vado Grant was reduced to 5,000 acres under private ownership. Massive barbed-wire enclosures on New Mexico lands had been built. By 1880, over one million miles of fencing closed off water resources and sheep trails. Scottish rancher Thomas Carson fenced off 100,000 acres in northern New Mexico, while Englishman Wilson Waddingham became a cattle baron with his extensive Bell Ranch. T.B. "Boss" Catron's law partner, William Joseph Mills, married Wilson Waddingham's daughter Alice. New Mexico and outside banks were funding speculative investments in cattle and lands. Syndicates were established for wealthy investors and speculators. Fifteen hundred British companies provided venture capital for investments in New Mexico lands. Fences were impeding access to rural churches, cemeteries, homes and even schools. In 1884, famous New Mexico sheriff Elfego Baca singlehandedly fought off eighty Texas cowboys who were busy terrorizing one Hispanic town.

During the late 1890s, Hispanic ranchers and farmers met in secret late at night in northern New Mexico. It started as a small group, but then the force steadily grew, reaching five thousand at its peak. The men met at certain locations, changing meeting places to avoid suspicion. At times, the gatherings took place in the town of Las Vegas, New Mexico, or at isolated ranches and villages. The purpose of the meetings was to discuss how to deal with vicious land, cattle and horse thieves who controlled the political and governmental systems in the territory. The plight of the people always fell on deaf ears. Land claims from rightful owners at times would take decades to process; in contrast, land speculator claims were processed in days or weeks. The Santa Fe Land Office served as a front for the notorious Santa Fe Ring.

Disenchantment in New Mexico

Right: Sometimes, burials took place at or near where someone had died on a land grant. This was prevalent during Indian attacks or war. Land thieves cared little. *Author's collection.*

Below: Santuario de Chimayo, a religious sanctuary where Native Hispanics went to pray for generations for the protection of their homes and lands. *Unknown photographer and date. Author's collection.*

No one would listen to the cries of residents. What further complicated the situation is that squatters from eastern states simply selected choice areas, built dwellings and, at times, stole what they wanted, including livestock and horses. Wealthy Americans did the same, but on a more massive scale. They could hire men to put up barbed-wire fences and no trespassing signs and to control the lands at the point of a gun. Helpless people whose families had owned the lands for generations were desperate.

The strongly Catholic people of New Mexico composed their own prayer for spiritual guidance from above during these trying times of land theft.

> *Maestro incomparable: Hemos tratado de balbucir algunas palabras para conocerte mejor y aprender la táctica de tus batallas...Acepta benignamente Nuestro esfuerzo pobre y da a Nuestra Patria raudales de aguas varias que ahoguen la sequia materialista de este siglo, que se quema lejos de ti.*

> *Incomparable Master: We have attempted to bumble some words to know you better and learn the tactics of your battles....Benignly accept our poor struggle and provide Our Country with abundant living waters that will drown out the material drought of this century that burns far from you.*

HARVEST OF TEARS

La Voz del Pueblo, El Abogado de Nuevo Mexico (the voice of the people, the attorney of New Mexico) was a Spanish-language newspaper located in Las Vegas, New Mexico. It not only provided a venue to learn about what was happening in Santa Fe and the territory; it was also a forum for people to speak out on pressing issues, including loss of lands. It was published from February 2, 1889, until at least 1915. Several issues are no longer extant. A local Hispanic rancher from northern New Mexico wrote an anonymous letter of unknown date, signed simply "P. and Don J." and written in Spanish, which he sent to the editor. The letter described the plight of the people of New Mexico. The following is part of the English translation:

> *A RANCHER....This voice will resonate, until it reaches the confines of the land because it consists of the adage, its strength is "The Voice of the people, is the Voice of God."...Think about ancient days, in Rome, when it was in eminent danger, or in a state of anarchy, when confusion and disorder reigned, when, it was attacked by a powerful enemy, naming a judicious and*

Disenchantment in New Mexico

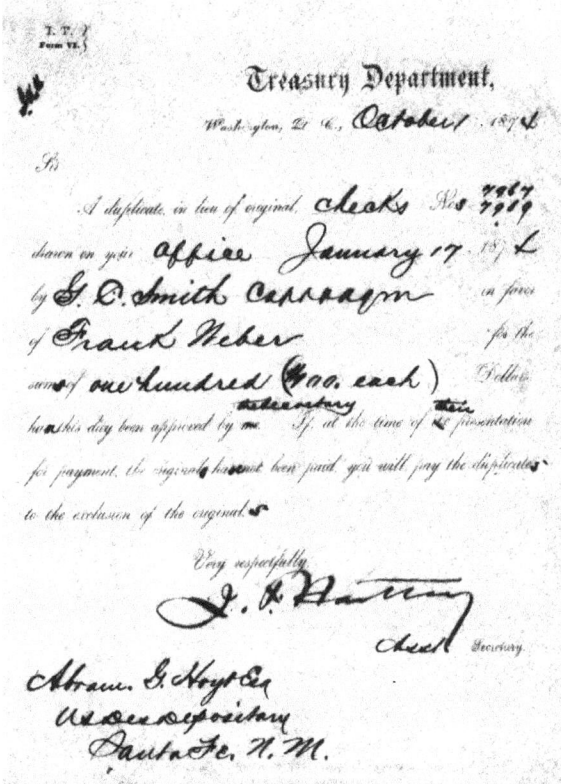

Those working for the U.S. government, including surveyors, received their pay through the U.S. Treasury Department. *Author's collection.*

honored dictator, saying what should be done and what everyone should obey. In this way, many Romans saved themselves from tremendous disasters and ruin. They always held their origin and impenetrable and blind ambition from those that governed them [those in command of our people and land] *are composed of all the birds of prey.... Vultures circling above, with their champion, a sure dictator that directs the political ship...asking for money, money...so they would have an abundance this year...pocketing the money, to advance his ranch and pasture-ground...thusly satisfying themselves with the defeated....The people are obligated to hear, see the suffering and be silent about certain disgraceful and repugnant dealings that are against the sentiments of a Christian people, simply because those that commit this, have money?...Be careful with these rank persons that are causing all sorts of trauma. I will bring all of this to light.*

Under the Treaty of Guadalupe Hidalgo, signed by the United States and Mexico on February 2, 1848, officially ending the Mexican-American

War, Mexico ceded approximately 234,000,000 acres to the United States. President Grover Cleveland sent a letter to George W. Julian on May 11, 1885, asking if he would accept the position of surveyor general for New Mexico Territory. President Cleveland was appalled with reports flowing into his office that land robbers, including many former Confederate officers and soldiers, were sweeping into the territory and capitalizing on land theft. He was concerned, as were others, that Confederate sympathizers and neo-Confederates would take over the West and bring about a resurgence of the Confederate states.

In 1912, when New Mexico became a state, two prominent members of the notorious Santa Fe Ring were elected to Congress. Albert Bacon Fall joined the infamous Thomas B. Catron, acknowledged leader of the Ring. All students of American government and history should be familiar with Senator Fall. His tenure involved one of the largest high-level corruption scandals in U.S. political history: the Tea Pot Dome Affair. A former secretary of the interior, Fall was charged with accepting bribes from oil companies in exchange for exclusive rights to drill for oil on federal land. His friend Catron became the largest landowner in the United States, controlling more than three million acres of Spanish/Mexican land grant property and Indian lands. He became a U.S. senator from New Mexico. While much of the American public have demanded that the names of former Confederates be erased from public buildings and Confederate statues removed, it is ironic that two counties in New Mexico are named for Lea and Catron, two infamous Confederate supporters and New Mexico land thieves.

5
CONTRAST IN LANDS

The Pueblo Indians seem to have been entitled under Spanish law to whatever lands they habitually occupied or used.
—John L. Kessell

The Native Americans had several names for the English and other Europeans on the East Coast, including the French, Dutch and, later, the Americans. Indians held that all of these groups made broken promises and broken treaties in their drive to expel Indians from their ancestral lands. Many tribes ceased to exist after the Pilgrims arrived to settle in 1620. Roy Cook, in his book *Thanksgiving: A Day of Mourning*, states:

> Most school children are taught that Native Americans helped the Pilgrims and were invited to the first Thanksgiving feast.... The conception of Native Americans gained from such early exposure is both inaccurate and potentially damaging to others.... Before the Pilgrims arrived Plymouth had been the site of a Pawtuxet village which was wiped out by a plague (introduced by English explorers looking to grab a piece of the New World land).... The pilgrims (who did not even call themselves pilgrims)...came here as part of a commercial venture. One of the very first things they did when they arrived on Cape Cod—before they even made it to Plymouth—was to rob Wampanoag graves at Corn Hill and steal as much of the Indians' winter provisions as they were able to carry.... The first official "Day of Thanksgiving" was proclaimed in 1637 by Massachusetts Governor John

New Mexico's Stolen Lands

Land speculators coveted lakes, fishing ponds, springs, artesian wells and all irrigable lands on Indian and Native Hispanic lands. *Photo by Ramón Juan Carlos de Aragón, 2001.*

> *Winthrop. He did so to celebrate the safe return of English colony men from Mystic, Connecticut. They massacred 600 Pequot that had laid down their weapons and accepted Christianity. Their new "brothers in Christ" rewarded them with a vicious and cowardly slaughter.*

It is still written jokingly that Manhattan Island was purchased from the Manhattan Indians for a few trinkets of glass beads that they marveled over. Historian Matt Soniak mentions that the Dutch National Archives contains a letter written on November 5, 1626, by Pieter Schage to the directors of the West India Company, stating that Peter Minuit and his colonists "have purchased the island of Manhattes from the savages for the value of 60 guilders." In fact, English colonizers stole not only lands from the Indians, but also their food. Patrick J. Kiger wrote:

> *North American colonists' warfare against Native Americans often was horrifyingly brutal. But one method they appear to have used shocks even*

more than all the bloody slaughter: The gifting of blankets and linens contaminated with smallpox....On July 13, Bouquet, who at that point was traveling across Pennsylvania with British reinforcements for Fort Pitt, responded to Amherst, promising that he would try to spread the disease to the Native Americans via contaminated blankets, "taking care however not to get the disease myself." That tactic seemed to please Amherst, who wrote back in approval on July 16, urging him to spread smallpox "as well as try every other method that can serve to Extirpate this Execreble [sic] *Race."*

The colonists confiscated provisions with claims that they had to ensure the survival of their own people. Many massacres of Indians took place. Water sources on their lands were purposely polluted, and entire settlements were burned to the ground—many men, women and children huddled in their homes dying in the process. Some remnants of tribes trying to escape the massacres and tortures managed to flee to Spanish-controlled areas; others escaped to isolated regions in Canada.

In New Mexico today, an annual celebration called the Gathering of Nations, or Pow Wow, takes place. This is a celebration of Native American culture, heritage and traditions through song, music and dance. Several Indian tribes take part and are represented. This very popular event showcases Indians for locals, tourists and travelers, who are awed by the ancient rituals. The first such event took place in 1921 in Gallup, New Mexico, a recognized center of the Navajo Nation. Newspapers around New Mexico promoted the "GREAT ALL-INDIAN SHOW." A forty-eight-page special edition of the *Gallup Independent* ("Western New Mexico's Daily Newspaper") was issued, produced by publisher A.W. Barnes. The news editor was J. Wesley Huff. Numerous articles of wide appeal to "Indian Enthusiasts" were written. The only writer who was credited was editor Huff, who wrote, "SHOW IS RUN WITH SPEED OF GREAT CIRCUS…EARLY preparations of the Ceremonial are made by M.L. 'Woodie' Woodward, secretary for the association of Gallup businessmen which manages Ceremonial affairs."

I remember as a child traveling from Las Vegas, New Mexico, to Albuquerque and seeing several multicolored billboards placed on both the south and north sides of what was then Highway 85. These read, "SEE REAL LIVE INDIANS—turn right or left to San Juan Ildefonso Pueblo."

The 25th Anniversary Ceremonial Edition of the *Gallup Independent* of August 12, 1946, is of particular interest, because the editors and writers demonstrated what the feelings of the general public were when considering Native Americans at the time of this event. Indians were meant not only to

Navajo land. An advertisement appeared on August 12, 1946, in a special edition of the *Gallup Independent* touting the attractiveness of Navajo Indians for tourists. *Author's collection.*

entertain people, but also to please them. J. Wesley Huff and his staff wrote an article titled "Ceremonial Is Reunion of Indian Tribes," describing in part the celebration:

> *While you are in Gallup for the 25th annual Inter-Tribal Indian Ceremonial discard your watch and plan to live as Indians do…the orange glow of the campfires against the white covers of the Navajo wagons, the rhythmic beat of the tom-toms, the shrill falsetto of the Navajo singers and the glowing round faces of the youngsters peering from their bedrolls…for it's a strange sight to be seen nowhere else in the United States.….Navajo, Apache, Hopi, Zuni, all of the Pueblo Indians from the Rio Grande Valley, Sioux, Kiowa, Shawnee, Cheyenne, Pawnee, and Shoshone from the Plains States, Seneca and Iroquois from the East and Paiute and Mission from the West…*

| 56TH CONGRESS, | HOUSE OF REPRESENTATIVES. | DOCUMENT |
| 1st Session. | | No. 302. |

LAND GRANT OF THE INDIANS OF THE PUEBLO OF ZUNI.

LETTER

FROM

THE SECRETARY OF THE INTERIOR,

TRANSMITTING

A COMMUNICATION FROM THE COMMISSIONER OF INDIAN AFFAIRS RECOMMENDING THAT THE LAND GRANT OF THE INDIANS OF THE PUEBLO OF ZUNI BE CONFIRMED TO THEM BY LEGISLATIVE ACT.

JANUARY 16, 1900.—Referred to the Committee on Indian Affairs and ordered to be printed.

DEPARTMENT OF THE INTERIOR,
Washington, January 15, 1900.

SIR: A grant of land was made September 25, 1689, by the Government of Spain to the Indians of the pueblo of Zuni, in the Territory of New Mexico.

Although in continuous possession of the lands for more than two hundred years, title in the Indians has never been confirmed. All the original deeds, documents, etc., covering the grant have been lost. Statements of this and other cases, with reports from the surveyor-general of New Mexico, through the Commissioner of the General Land Office, were submitted by the Department on December 11, 1880, to the Speaker of the House of Representatives for Congressional action, but no action thereon seems to have been taken by the Congress.

The matter is now presented by the Commissioner of Indian Affairs with recommendation for early action on the long-delayed though recognized right of these Indians to the land covered by the said grant.

A similar grant to the Indians of the pueblo of Santa Ana was confirmed by the act of Congress approved February 9, 1869 (15 Statutes, 438), which seems to be a precedent for favorable action in this instance. (Attention is invited to House Report No. 70, Fortieth Congress, second session, for the facts in the case of the Santa Ana grant.)

The Supreme Court of the United States at the October term, 1899, in The United States, appellant, *v.* J. Francisco Chavez and Pueblo of

Pueblo Indian lands were subject to confirmation by Congress. All Pueblo Indians lost much of their ancestral lands, as did other tribes in New Mexico. *Author's collection.*

mysterious and entrancing, holding you to your seat to the last as the wild Navajos, bathing their clay-daubed bodies with blazing torches of cedar bark turn the arena into a bedlam of fiery motion.

Another *Gallup Independent* story, "Navajo Treaty Signed a Century Ago," described a treaty negotiated between the Americans and the Navajo Indians. It was written:

> *Colonel Doniphan Met 14 Chiefs at Bear Spring.... The first Treaty between the United States and the Navajo Nation was reached just 100 years ago in November when Colonel Doniphan of the first Missouri Volunteers met with the chiefs of "The People" at Bear Springs, west of Gallup.... The Treaty was signed by Doniphan and others of his command on behalf of President James K. Polk and no less than 14 Navajo headmen.... The ceremony which followed a long series of parades, feasts and dancing, was impressive. After it was over Doniphan made a detour to Zuni Pueblo and signed with them a treaty also. It was worth a little more than the Navajo Treaty, for the Zunis were less warlike....With Price's Second Missouri, the "Mormon Battalion," coming to garrison Santa Fe, Kearny ordered Doniphan to pacify the Indians and then march to Chihuahua which General Wool was supposed to be occupying.*

The so-called Mormon Battalion was nothing more than a few hundred Mormon families attempting to escape torture and abuse in Missouri. The Mormons felt they would be much safer in Mexican territory from the prejudice, including the terrible racial and sexual abuse they were experiencing in the states. Kearny allowed the men to wear regular clothing and to travel with their wives and children in an effort to fool New Mexican forces into thinking it was merely a migrant group desiring to reach California to colonize and settle. His ruse temporarily worked. Kearny sent orders to Doniphan:

> *To put teeth in the pacification—to invade the Navajo country, to release captives, reclaim stolen property and awe or beat the Indians into submission. The job set for the first Missouri was a tough one for a band of farm boy volunteers. They had done pretty well so far. They had added many thousands of miles to the United States; had established an advanced post which made the Conquest of California secure; and seemed to have conciliated a conquered people. From now on their work was prodigious....*

They [the Missourians] *were supposed to be cavalry, but their horses were half starved and their pack mules were in no better condition. At the end of the journey they had about half as many of each as they had started with. Their boots had not been replaced. Nothing like a uniform was left. They were dressed in native New Mexican or Indian costumes… they labored through many miles of snow up to their waist, and had to scrounge in the snow for firewood—but they found none. NO WONDER the Navajo they met agreed to come to Bear Spring to talk peace. They could have massacred this band of adventurers in a few minutes at their ease and with complete impunity. The Navajo had not heard before that there were white men like these.… Captain Reid took his detachment into the heart of the Navajo country, the Chaska Mountains and Laguna, Colorado, at their base, and had rounded up to five hundred awed Navajo.*

In English and American history, there is a long record of broken treaties and promises. A major reason for continuous attempts to squeeze the Indians out of their shrinking lands was the pressure imposed on the government by those desiring to move into the rich lands of the Indians. Once gold, other precious metals and minerals were discovered on Native American–controlled lands, any excuse was fomented to battle the Indians and remove them from their ancient ancestral lands—lands they had held for thousands of years. Although the Treaty of Guadalupe Hidalgo, ending the Mexican-American War, had been signed, guaranteeing the rights of land ownership to the inhabitants of Mexican territories, Americans firmly believed this treaty did not apply to the Indians. Under the American government, Indians, essentially, had no rights. An additional article in the *Gallup Independent*, "Navajo Treaty Signed a Century Ago," continued with the following:

VANISHING (?) AMERICANS DEMANDING THEIR RIGHTS.…
IF YOUR mental picture of an Indian is a cross between a half naked, painted medicine man, and a shiftless, blanket-wrapped ne'er do-well living in a sort beneficent concentration camp called a reservation on the bounty of the government, you'd better throw it away. All Indians today are citizens, if they were born in the United States [Native Americans lived in the country before it became the United States], *by virtue of the citizenship act of 1924. They may leave and return to their reservations at will. They vote…some are industrious, some are lazy…some tribes, of course, have virtually disappeared. The famous Iroquois Confederacy, once so powerful and outstanding among all Indian peoples, is now dispersed.*

New Mexico's Stolen Lands

Drawing of Chief Geronimo by Rosa María Calles. Tribal chiefs Victorio, Cochise, Manuelito, Sitting Bull, Geronimo and others desperately fought for their ancestral lands. *Author's collection.*

Most of the Mohawks, Cayuga's, and Onondagas now live in Canada. The Seneca live on several reservations in New York State and one in Oklahoma, and there are also small reservations for the remaining Tuscarora, Onondagas and Mohawks, while the Oneidas in the United States have a reservation in New York and one in Wisconsin.... THE SOUTHERN plains Indians now live in Oklahoma, a part of which was formerly the Indian Territory, to which Indians from many states were forced to move.... The great majority are farmers, although some lease their lands, and some no longer have lands.... Many treaty provisions still stand, making a curious hodge-podge of treaty law, federal legislation, and custom. In an effort to make the treaties intelligible to what was regarded as an inferior and savage race, and to convince a people utterly innocent of our legalities that these promises were binding and eternal, picturesque language was employed.... LET THE Red children of the Great White Father, the treaties read, retire beyond a certain line, let them live in amity with their white brethren, and they should be left in peace "as long as the rivers shall run and the grass shall grow." Not so long ago, as a result of the white man's greed and ignorance, the rivers ceased to run and the grass to grow in the southwestern dust bowl, but the white man, ever eager for more and more land, had breached the treaties countless times before this natural phenomenon provided an excuse....CONVERSELY, this treaty relationship imposed upon the Indian—and still imposes, to a lesser degree—a certain legal inferiority....An Indian tribe may not bring a suit against the government in the Court of Claims unless Congress passes a special act permitting it to do so....Denial of the vote to Indians in Arizona and New Mexico is an indirect outgrowth of treaty provisions. In Arizona, the right of suffrage is denied to Indians on the ground that Indians are within the provision of the state constitution denying suffrage to persons under guardianship, and in New Mexico, on grounds of non-taxation. Lands held by the Government in trust for the Indians are held to be government property, and therefore not subject to state taxation. However, an Indian may, for all legal purposes, cease to be an Indian whenever he wants, simply by giving up his tribal membership. By this act he relieves the Government of any responsibility toward him under terms of tribal treaties....UNTIL 1949, the administration of Indian Affairs was a military function, exercised by men to whom, for the most part, a good Indian was a dead Indian. It still might be so, except that it got too expensive....So Indian affairs were placed under the newly created Interior Department. Then, casting about for a legal way to deprive the Indian of his lands, someone hit on the brilliant "allotment" scheme. It was argued that if each Indian had a piece of land to call his own, it would aid in making him over into an imitation of a white man, through pride of ownership....

When someone—in 1815—found gold at Dahlonega, Georgia, on the edge of the Cherokee reservation, the Indians were squeezed out....The Indians put up some resistance and even those who went along willingly, suffered, a quarter of them dying. When only 1,000 holdouts were left of the original 16,000 the government made a deal. The leader of the fugitive Indians gave himself up to be executed, in return for a small reservation in the western part of North Carolina, where now his descendants try to scrabble out a living on mountain sides....After each Indian had his piece of land, which he was forbidden to sell for 25 years, the remaining Indian lands were declared "surplus" and opened up to white settlement....The allotment system succeeded in "checker boarding" the reservations, leaving the Indian no recourse but to lease his land to large cattle companies for a few cents an acre a year....The Indians thus driven from their land, congregated *close to their agencies, living in shanties and forming rural slums. The fresh air and open life of the teepee was traded for the stench of bodies huddled about an iron stove in an airless shack. Food was scarce. Tuberculosis to which the Indian is peculiarly subject took a terrific toll....THE INDIAN was discouraged in the practice of his religion, his tribal culture, even his handicraft....Indian children were taught to ridicule the wisdom of their parents....They were forbidden to speak their native tongue....Even when he succeeded in getting into the white men's courts, capricious decisions made a mockery of the simple justice the Indian sought. When the Paiute Indians on the Warm Springs Reservation in Oregon got into a court a year or so ago with a boundary dispute, the court held that although the boundary was where the Indians said it was, and that the Government had taken Indian land for a national forest still, the Government had contributed money towards the Indian's support, the Indians should forfeit the land. In 1920, the Government was holding trust for the Blackfoot Indians some $3,000,000 from leases, sales of timber, and sales of land from their reservation. Seven years later, there was $25,000 left, nor was any good accounting to be found. The Great White Father had spent the rest on "administrative costs," salaries and maintenance for white men.*

Chief Sitting Bull of the Lakota Hunkpapa tribe fearlessly led his people in a long struggle to protect their ancient lands. He declared, "They claim this mother of ours, the Earth, for their own use, and fence the neighbors away from her, and deface her with buildings and their refuse....If we must die we die defending our rights....They want us to give up another large piece of our tribal land. This is not the first time or the last time."

An editorial appeared in the *Daily Citizen* (Albuquerque, New Mexico) on Thursday, January 15, 1891. Major C.E. Vandever, once a Navajo agent, declared that accounts appearing in the newspaper describing the Navajo gold fields in the Carrizo Mountains were not an exaggeration. It read:

Agent Vandever informed THE CITIZEN that he has received within the last ten days, a letter from the commissioner of Indian affairs, in which that officer states that he has recommended to the secretary of the interior the opening of that portion of the reservation. This is done not only for the purpose of giving the miner and prospector an opportunity to take out the riches which abound in that district, but also to protect the Indians, because it is perfectly clear that enterprising white men cannot long be kept out of this region....To give the Indians land that they

Disenchantment in New Mexico

Lands in New Mexico Territory were claimed by the government, homesteaders, squatters and mining claim jumpers. Volcano lava hills and desert lands were wanted. *Photo by Rosa María Calles, 2015.*

> *can use, in some other part of the country, and then open this district to American enterprise, would certainly be a wise policy on the part of the government, because the Indians care nothing for the mines, and as the district is of no value for any other purpose, it is practically useless to them; and because when its wealth becomes known, it will be impossible for the Indian agent, or even the United States government to keep people out of it. There is no doubt of the fact that the Carrizo mountain country is one of the richest gold districts ever yet discovered in the United States.... The Carrizo Mountains are too rich in gold to remain long in possession of savages who will make no use of them.*

After the horrendous "Long Walk," when the Navajo tribe endured a tortuous journey to Bosque Redondo conducted by the U.S. Cavalry led by Colonel Christopher "Kit" Carson, for whom the Carson National Forest is named, they became displaced. Navajos were forcefully removed from their ancestral lands, which had been guaranteed by the Treaty of Guadalupe Hidalgo and signed by the United States and Mexico. Navajo Indians were interred in what natives called a "concentration camp." During the death march, many Navajo starved to death or were shot because they could not keep up with the rest of the tribe. This event is one of the blackest pages in U.S. history. They were then placed in a reservation on land that government officials felt quite assured was useless. But when gold was found, they were forcefully removed once again, to another area. Eventually, uranium was discovered on the new Navajo lands, a mineral essential for the production of nuclear energy and weapons. The Navajo now reside in a desert area under miserable conditions.

SAN ILDEFONSO PUEBLO AND CHIEF BIBO

Besides some Americans moving into New Mexico seeking a new life, there were many vain and gold-hungry opportunists. These included lawyers, bankers, shifty carpetbaggers and shady merchants once called snake-oil peddlers. The U.S. government posted positions for Indian traders and agents in New Mexico. The Bibo brothers arrived to stake their claims. In their home country of Germany, the Bibo family had heard about the limitless opportunities in the American West and the boundless lands of New Mexico.

Nathan, Simon and Joseph Bibo at first worked for the German-Jewish Spiegelbergs in the capital city of Santa Fe. Ironically, the Spiegelberg family had traveled along with Colonel Stephen Watts Kearny and his

Las Vegas, New Mexico bank receipt. Many banks sprang up in New Mexico to service American and English investors depositing funds to develop stolen lands. *Author's collection.*

Missouri volunteers in 1846 during the invasion of New Mexico. Similarly to other Jewish emigrants, the Bibos saw the vast opportunities for capitalizing that were available in the territory, so they went their own way once the Spiegelbergs provided them with funds. The Bibo brothers established a trading post at Laguna Pueblo. Younger brother Solomon joined his brothers in 1869. By this time, Simon and Nathan were involved in securing government contracts to provide beef and other commodities to various forts, including Fort Defiance and Fort Wingate, plus other U.S. military outposts in western New Mexico and eastern Arizona. The Bibo brothers became actively involved in trading with the Indian pueblos and the Navajo. Because of the enormous profits that were being gained, Nathan Bibo opened a mercantile in Bernalillo, New Mexico. His brothers Solomon and Simon did the same on the Cebolleta Land Grant. This grant was eventually stolen through fraud and deceit. The Cebolleta Land Grant and the village of Cebolleta were located just north of Laguna Pueblo. The idea behind this move was to establish a base for trading with the Navajo Indians.

Solomon Bibo traveled along the Santa Fe Trail and joined Simon in Cebolleta. In time, he made his way into other Indian pueblos after helping his brothers at Laguna. Solomon discovered that Acoma Pueblo

American immigrants flooded into New Mexico from the East on the Santa Fe Trail. Land hunger needed to be quenched. Land thieves moved in. *Unknown engraver and date. Author's collection.*

was embroiled in a land dispute with the Laguna Indians. The Acoma Indians had laid claim to several hundred thousand acres of ancestral lands. In 1877, through a signed treaty with the U.S. government, they were confirmed 94,000 acres, much to the disdain of Acoma Pueblo elders. Historical evidence went back to both the Mexican and Spanish governments in Santa Fe. The Acomas had a documented chain of title. They especially trusted Solomon, because they had an age-old disdain for the Spanish and their descendants. Solomon successfully capitalized on this, telling them that all of their problems had to do with the Spanish and, especially, the Mexicans.

The U.S. Department of the Interior, through the New Mexico surveyor general, conducted a survey of Acoma Pueblo Indian lands between 1876 and 1877. Due to complaints initiated by the Acoma, there was a review of the survey in 1881. The deputy surveyors were brothers Walter and Robert Marmon. Both were Presbyterian missionaries assigned to Laguna Pueblo, which also laid claim to the disputed lands. The two brothers were also traders, and both of them married into the pueblo, thus creating a vested interest. As a result, the disputed lands were awarded to the Laguna Indians. Soon after this, Solomon Bibo appealed in 1882 to the commissioner of the Bureau of Indian Affairs to provide him with a license to trade with the Acoma Indians and establish a trading post on their pueblo. The license was granted. After two years in business at the pueblo, Bibo convinced the tribe that he was in a position with the U.S. government to protect their lands so that no more of it would be taken away. In addition to this protection, Bibo promised he would pay the Acoma Indians $12,000, protect their cattle, keep trespassers and those bent on stealing their lands away and pay them $0.10 per ton of coal that would be mined from their lands, all in exchange for a thirty-year lease to him. Hiram Price, the commissioner of Indian affairs, through the intervention of the U.S. Indian agent at Santa Fe, negated the lease and its arrangements.

Solomon Bibo would not give up. He converted to the Catholic faith and married Juana Valle, the granddaughter of the former Acoma governor, in a ceremony before the Catholic priest at the Acoma mission church on May 1, 1885. He followed this up with a civil ceremony before a justice of the peace and recorded this on August 30, 1885. Bibo wanted to secure any rights that could arise through this marriage, which officially made him a member of the Acoma tribe, much as had been done for Robert and Walter Marmon at Laguna Pueblo. Two things occurred. First, Bibo

Disenchantment in New Mexico

The ancient San Ildefonso Pueblo and the peaceful Indians residing there fell prey to American Indian agents and traders. They bartered pennies for Native American artworks to sell to tourists. *Unknown photographer, circa 1909.*

succeeded and was appointed as governor of Acoma Pueblo by American government officials. It is claimed that pueblo elders also supported this appointment and his election as chief of their tribe, which went against all of Native American history and tradition. Second, Bibo decided to take up cattle ranching and secured a grazing lease from the tribe, which he initiated. The U.S. Indian agent accused Solomon Bibo of continuing to defraud the tribe; his trading license was revoked. A Catholic priest printed and distributed a broadside accusing Bibo of attempting to steal Cebolleta Land Grant lands. He was called *Un Israelita Rico* ("a rich Israelite") attempting to defraud true heirs of the land grant. The Bibo brothers even attempted to set up their own town on the land grant, called Bibo, New Mexico. Multiple controversies surround Solomon Bibo and his tenure in tribal leadership. Seeing the writing on the wall, he moved his family to San Francisco, California, far away from possible legal repercussions that continued to haunt him. He saw California as another area of opportunity. Solomon Bibo died in 1934, ten years later.

Reservation Land

If you can't change them, absorb them until they simply disappear into the mainstream culture....In Washington's infinite wisdom, it was decided that tribes should no longer be tribes, never mind that they had been tribes for thousands of years.
—Ben Nighthorse Campbell, U.S. senator, Colorado

In a letter from U.S. surveyor general William Pelham to U.S. commissioner of the Land Office Thomas A. Hendricks, dated May 27, 1856, the surveyor wrote:

> *I have been informed that designing and mischievous individuals having intercourse with many of the Pueblo Indians of this territory, have been endeavoring to impress this simple minded though worthy people with the belief that the object of the Government in demanding the title papers to their lands is to destroy such evidence of title they possess and then withhold Patents. The consequence is the Indians having no other evidence of title than the documents made by the Spanish Government, feel and express an unwillingness to surrender their papers for the purpose of being sent to Washington as required.*

On January 6, 1879, Indian Agent Isaiah Walker wrote a letter from the Lyandothe (Wyandotte) Reservation to M.W. Browne and Francisco Antonio Manzanares in Las Vegas, New Mexico. The Wyandotte Indians, or the Wendot Confederacy, had been moved from the Georgian Bay and Lake Huron region to Oklahoma. After they were placed on a reservation, Kansas City annexed some of the Indian land. On August 1, 1956, the U.S. Congress passed a law to terminate the tribe under the Federal Termination Act. This policy was meant to assimilate all Indians into the American mainstream. As far back as 1897, various individuals, including Walker, attempted to develop ideas as to how they could get reservation land. Methods of assimilation were already taking place. Isaiah Walker expected some problems along the way but also felt that the final outcome would be in his favor. He had already received one answer and mentioned a reply from George Cove of the General Land Office in Santa Fe. He said, "I am not surprised at the reply. As I have such one from the Commissioner of Indian Affairs, and do not expect a favorable one...until sending me a copy of the case from the U.S. Supreme Court Reports giving a full reference to the

Disenchantment in New Mexico

Indians and Indian agents, along with troops, gathered for the signing of treaties. Most treaties were broken when circumstances demanded it. *Courtesy New Mexico Historical Society.*

case. Showing how the location and patenting had been overlooked by the decisions. Then and then only will get a satisfactory reply."

It can be surmised by Walker's next letter, written from the Lyandothe Reservation in Indian Territory to M.W. Browne of Las Vegas concerning the acquisition of a land grant and Indian lands, that his next approach was to claim he would mine the land he was requesting from the government. Walker had met a Mr. Pinckney, who carried a letter of introduction. According to the letter, Pinckney had left on the train for New Mexico Territory to check up on the Rio Mine somewhere in New Mexico "to defend the location of Float….I am quite sure he knows his business, and if as he says…can make the location stick." What Walker referred to was gold dust or placer gold. This was gold found in streams and in southern New Mexico in Indian Territory and in grant lands. Many Americans panning for gold on those lands became wealthy. Walker goes on to mention a Mr. Robinson, who was apparently venturing in on this business. He added, "He came none too soon as I had about sold the float and am now waiting to get a reply from the commissioner [U.S. land commissioner in Santa Fe]…as to locating in the Territory of New Mexico and Indian Territory…as there are no known claimants, or settlers to contend with."

Isaiah Walker went on to note that he had contacted J.P. Long, his attorney, in New Mexico to draw up and execute papers in Pinckney's name, which would be satisfactory. Apparently, Pinckney was supplying the money for the venture. Walker mentioned a Nicholas who may have been a partner in the sale. He asked of Browne:

> *I want you to remit by draft less the price amount paid $1,000 one thousand dollars with interest after one year and a reasonable commission for what you have done for us and return the original papers so that I may be able to surrender it to Long. He has made absolute conveyance to Robinson....I hope he* [Nicholas] *will not object to what I have done, as I regard the price obtained $5.00 five dollars per acre as good now as when we sold to you.*

A man named Joseph "Joe" Gentry sent an undated note to E.V. Long, now Judge E.V. Long: "Dear Judge, Am enclosing clippings from paper regarding title of land as you have always handled my Land Business." Gentry may have had strong connections with politicians, because Long immediately sent a communication to the governor, who may have been Governor Edmund G. Ross. The judge wrote the governor: "I am writing Mr. Gentry that I have turned this over to you. Please see just how this is and write him without fail....Do not neglect for one moment." Elisha V. Long was well placed with the Santa Fe Ring and became chief of the New Mexico Territorial Supreme Court.

A Celebration

On the Fourth of July in 1876, one hundred years after the founding of the United States, a commemoration was held in Santa Fe. It is ironic that those who spearheaded the momentous event were members of the Santa Fe Ring, including a former governor. William Frederich Malton Arny had served as an Indian agent. Besides being an organizer of the New Mexico event, Arny also represented the territory at the huge Centennial Exposition, which also took place in 1876 in Philadelphia. The "Centennial" booklet published a list of all of the noted dignitaries, including Catron and C.H. Gildersleave, noted land thieves exposed by investigator George W. Julian.

Disenchantment in New Mexico

Wealthy Americans loved the Spanish architecture and the beehive ovens of Moorish origin in New Mexico. They built lavish homes, now called "Santa Fe style." *Unknown photographer, circa 1945. Author's collection.*

The Centennial Celebration was held in Santa Fe, New Mexico, on July 4, 1876. The commemoration booklet listed: "Toasts and Sentiments by H.M. Atkinson, Surveyor General; Honorable John Pratt, Marshall; General Edward Hatch, Military Commander of the District of New Mexico; Honorable T.B. Catron, District Attorney; E.A. Fisqe, Esquire, C.H. Gildersleeve, Esquire. Centennial Poem by A.Z. Higgins, Esquire."

In 1876, a pamphlet was issued featuring ex-Governor W.F.M. Arny's oration published by Williams & Shaw and printed in Santa Fe. Governor Arny wrote a historical sketch, and his section on mines and mining in New Mexico is particularly relevant to land theft in New Mexico:

> *I will endeavor briefly to set forth that of the Territory itself as to mines and mining. The subject is one of great interest....Since the massacre of the Spaniards by the Pueblo Indians in 1680 all the richest mines have been covered by them....The "City of Holy Faith," is surrounded with the precious metals....The following I quote from Professor Raymond's report for 1870, in which he says: "The Cerrillos, 17 miles southwest of Santa Fe, contain many silver bearing lodes which have been described, although they are well worth it. They are situated on an old Spanish grant belonging*

An Isleta Pueblo funeral. For generations, Pueblo Indians and nearby Native Hispanic residents maintained friendly relations. Both communities shared water for farming. *Author's collection.*

to the Baca y Delgado family." (These lands have since been surveyed as public lands and sold by the government to citizens who are now working the mines.)...Many other mines and lodes of gold and silver could be mentioned, but the time allotted to me on this occasion will not permit... the crowd of Pueblo Indians (under charge of Governor Arny)—a band

> *of about a hundred grotesque looking creatures—men, women and children, dressed in their peculiar Indian costumes, and many of them bearing the wares of their home manufacture.... The amusement committee had put up a tall smooth and well-greased pole in the street....As the band music progressed the Indians struck up a lively air on their peculiar primitive instruments, with their "war dance" accompaniment, and the old men of the Pueblos procured several large lard cans for musical instruments, and getting together the women, youths, and children, commenced what they called their "corn dance," a lively sinuous procedure of shuffling of feet, clapping of hands, curtsying...until about six o'clock, when the Pueblo Indians went for the greased pole.... The first Indians attempt [to reach the top] was a failure; the second ditto; the third likewise, and so on until about a dozen had pretty well wiped the grease off to about halfway to the top, when they concluded to try strategy. One fellow would start up, when they would "boost" him, until about a half a dozen were strung along, clinging to their slippery perch, when the bottom man would lose his grip and the whole party come scooting to the bottom in a bunch. Then another party tried sand, and the top man would carry up sand in his shirt tail and throw it above him on the pole as he slowly went up, rubbing off the grease at the same time; in this way after much labor the top was reached.*

According to writers, all had a good time as whiskey, wine and beer flowed freely, with plentiful cigars shared by onlookers. Indians and Mexicans provided the amusement, to the delight of everyone who celebrated the Fourth of July centennial in the capital city of Santa Fe in 1876.

6

MOVED BY GREED

A group of Catholic men and women called the Hermanos and Hermanas Penitentes, a lay order of penitents in New Mexico, suddenly found themselves victims of religious persecution from intolerant American immigrants and a newly appointed American prelate.

During and after the defeat of Mexico in the Mexican-American War, Catholicism was under attack in those former Mexican, now U.S. territory. English and American history is replete with incidents of disdain and intolerance toward the Catholic faith and its believers and their priests. In fact, at one time in New England, the killing of priests as well as Indians went unpunished. The noble idea of freedom of religion for the most part did not apply to Roman Catholics, Mormons and those of other faiths, such as Islam and, in general, non-Protestants. Once New Mexico officially became a territory of the United States, migration into this area followed. What would eventually be known as the American Catholic Church, often at extreme odds with the Holy See at the Vatican, emerged. It was obvious that this uniquely American Catholic Church would view New Mexico not only as a defeated and conquered territory (it included all of Arizona and parts of Colorado, Nevada and California) but also as land ripe for American missionary zeal, as proclaimed by "Manifest Destiny."

In 1850, Frenchman Jean Baptiste Lamy, an obscure priest with little history or accomplishments and disliked by the German parishioners he served in Kentucky, was proclaimed Vicar Apostolic as Bishop of Agathonica by Pope Pius IX. In his decree, the pope unwittingly failed to notify church officials

A German newspaper advertisement touts "Air Line" railroad excursions from St. Louis to New Mexico and other destinations. German immigrants were to consider availability of lands, including Indian Territory. *Author's collection.*

in Mexico about changes of ecclesiastical authority as a result of the U.S. conquest and the Republic of Mexico, along with its people, vanquishing. Lamy was immortalized as a hero in Willa Cather's famous American novel *Death Comes for the Archbishop*. In her historical fictional novel, Cather pretty much reflected the American sentiments against Mexico of the period. Bishop Lamy, fictionalized as Bishop Latour, was sent out by the church as a missionary into a wild, immoral and deplorable territory to bring faith to an uncivilized world of Indian heathens and Mexican profligates. This was also the picture depicted for the pope in Rome. In truth, far from Cather's fictionalized heroic portrayal of Lamy, he had a much darker side, as he joined other American opportunists in New Mexican land theft.

Jean Baptiste Lamy was born in Lempdes, France, on October 11, 1814. His father served as the mayor of Lempdes. Lamy attended a Jesuit college in 1823. He began preparing for the priesthood at the seminary of Claremont in 1831. In 1832, he entered the Mont-Ferrand Seminary, which was run by Sulpician priests. It was at this seminary that Lamy would meet his lifelong friend Joseph Projectus Machebeuf. In 1838, both Lamy and Machebeuf were ordained as priests. They were both assigned to the United States of America as missionaries. Father Lamy would not only depend on Father Machebeuf but would also always confide in him, even when his friend consistently broke the laws of the church. Needless to say, both young priests spoke only French and the Latin they needed for church services. This would cause problems for them in America, especially when they were assigned to a parish. Masses were conducted in Latin, but there was virtually no interaction with parishioners except through English interpreters.

Lamy was assigned to a German parish. He complained that the German parishioners were not paying their required tithes, which was needed to provide for a new church. After the German Catholics complained, he was assigned to a parish in Covington, Kentucky. Meanwhile, American bishops gathered in council in Baltimore, Maryland. They requested that the pope form a new bishopric within previously held Mexican territory. Pius IX named Father Lamy to a new post on July 29, 1853. Lamy and Father Machebeuf immediately set out for New Mexico. Once he finally arrived in New Mexico, Lamy set out to lay claim to his position and also to what he would consider church lands.

Lamy's dream was to replace the mud "hovel" adobe churches of New Mexico with worthy French-style edifices. To realize his dream, mandatory tithing and church fees for services would be required. A cathedral worthy

Disenchantment in New Mexico

Descanso. When mourners carried coffins for burial at land grant cemeteries, they erected crosses at resting places. Both descansos and cemeteries were lost to land developers, circa 1940. *Author's collection.*

of Lamy's new position that rivaled those of Europe and France was finally built. Lamy appointed Father Machebeuf, whom he had brought along as the new vicar general of New Mexico Territory. Although Bishop Jean Batiste Lamy gave an accounting of the number of Catholics in the territory, the number steadily started to dwindle. There were several reasons for this, such as exorbitant tithing, intolerance toward Hispanic and Native American cultures and his high-handed ways. To accomplish his grandiose plans, Lamy began to employ various unorthodox methods. Vicar Juan Felipe Ortiz in Santa Fe left to consult with his previous superior, José Antonio Laureano de Zubiria y Escalante, in Durango, Mexico, about pressing matters, including, possibly, that Ortiz felt he himself had been appointed as the new bishop. Bishop Zubiria had already informed New Mexico's priests to submit to Lamy's episcopal authority. Zubiria admitted in a letter that he had not been officially informed by the pope and Vatican concerning any change in his administrative position in the church in New Mexico but that Lamy had shown him papers and that he was ready to turn his authority over to the American Catholic Church.

The mystery and intrigue start here. A leading newspaper in Ohio, the *Cincinnati Catholic Telegraph*, ran a story on July 29, 1853, claiming that the pope had named a new bishop of Santa Fe, in New Mexico: Vicar Don Juan

Felipe Ortiz, who had served as vicar of the church for many years. The *Catholic Herald* also announced Vicar Juan Felipe Ortiz as the new bishop of Santa Fe. In New Mexico, the *Santa Fe Gazette* picked up the story on November 26, 1853. The *Baltimore Catholic Mirror* in Maryland countered these glaring announcements by naming Lamy as the new bishop. Lamy quickly had the *Santa Fe Gazette* print a retraction. No one knows when parchment "bulls" from the pope with leaden seals arrived in Santa Fe to formally announce Lamy's appointment, or what became of them. Vicar Don Juan Felipe Ortiz demanded to see the documents. Lamy refused and wrote to Bishop John Baptist Purcell in Cincinnati: "Vicar Ortiz had the humility to propose himself to Rome as Bishop of the Diocese and to have us suspended or at least removed. This very week he wrote me an insolent letter, asking me to show him a document of the sovereign Pontife [sic] by which I could prove that I was authorized to take this parish."

Other New Mexico priests followed suit in asking to see Lamy's papers. The new American bishop was outraged! Bishop Jean Baptiste Lamy appealed to the American military for protection and to American political officials and the courts for support. He received it. In his first census of New Mexico, Lamy wrote that he found "sixty eight thousand Catholics, two thousand heretics, and close to forty thousand infidels."

While Vicar Ortiz was gone from Santa Fe, Lamy rapidly moved in and set himself up at the St. Francis Church and took over Ortiz's properties. He also took over rich farmlands he claimed were part of the property associated with the previous military chapel. The military chapel was meant for Santa Fe's presidio encampment and for soldiers stationed there. Governor Francisco Marín del Valle built the chapel in 1760. It was the property of Spain's military ordinariate, under a separate bishop's jurisdiction. It continued with these same terms under the government of Mexico. However, when Colonel Kearny took over Santa Fe in the name of the U.S. government, the military chapel fell into his hands. Lamy was successful in claiming the chapel and properties in the name of the Catholic Church and, in turn, sold some of the holdings to Jewish merchant Levi Spiegelberg. La Castrense was torn down in the name of progress. New Mexico's famous Governor Don Diego de Vargas was most probably buried there along with other famous New Mexicans from the Spanish colonial and Mexican periods. This meant nothing to Lamy.

Bishop Lamy then began to lay claim to other private chapels, oratorios, Penitente *moradas* (private chapels) and accompanying lands it is now admitted he had no rights to. Lamy named Father Machebeuf as vicar

Mountain sheep camps turned to ruins when Native Hispanic shepherds and their flocks were forced out of common lands taken over by the U.S. government. *Photo by Rosa María Calles, 2009.*

general. When Vicar Ortiz returned, he was stunned not only by Lamy's assertions but also by his actions. His family had built the Rosario Chapel of La Conquistadora, Our Lady of Santa Fe, to house the famous wooden statue brought to New Mexico around 1624 and removed for safekeeping during the Pueblo Indian Revolt of 1680. De Vargas returned it in triumph around 1692. The well-known annual Fiesta de Santa Fe celebrates La Conquistadora, translated as the Conqueror of Souls, as Nuestra Señora de la Santa Fe, or our Lady of the Holy Faith. The famous San Miguel Church, or chapel, recognized as one of the earliest churches built in the United States, was privately constructed and did not belong to the new diocese. Our Lady of Guadalupe Chapel, now a church, built sometime after 1800 by land grant devotees, was also claimed by Lamy as church property. Residents protested. Lamy took the issue to court and fiercely threatened excommunication from the church for those who opposed him. Civil War hero Lieutenant Colonel Manuel Antonio Chávez, who defeated the Confederates at the famous Battle of Glorieta, along with his troops, strongly opposed Lamy's actions. Presumed bishop Lamy stated that he would cast those who opposed him out of the church.

As quickly as he could, Lamy replaced more than 90 percent of New Mexico's Mexican clergy with French priests. He retained those who did not question him and those who followed his precepts. To his credit, he did introduce French nuns into the territory. They opened up schools, which charged tuition for attendance. Lamy had these groups of nuns pay for properties he sold them. Tuition charges paid for the properties and buildings. Priest orders such as the Jesuits were also required to pay him for properties he claimed but did not rightfully own. It is recorded in history that both Catholic schools and American Protestant schools punished children for speaking Spanish. Indian children and their parents were required to adapt to American ways and to the English language, as they were forced to forget their indigenous and native cultures. Eventually, public schools followed suit.

In a short history of Belen, *Seminario de Nuestra Señora de Guadalupe, Belen, New Mexico*, published by the Ward Anderson Printing Company in 1930, the Servite priests mentioned a particularly interesting incident of December 1856. Lamy was faced with yet another of a multitude of problems. The bishop wanted the old adobe church at Belen, New Mexico, which had been built in the eighteenth century, torn down and replaced with a more acceptable church. The residents protested, saying they would repair it. Lamy countered with, "all who persist in their intentions of rebuilding the old church, or of retaining the sacred vessels, statues, etcetera, shall be excommunicated, and any priest who should say Mass in the church will be suspended." He added that if any parishioner or priest should ask for forgiveness, Lamy would retract suspensions and excommunications.

MORE AMERICAN IMMIGRANTS

Migration into New Mexico had been taking place for several decades. Some of the reasons for this can be found in unusual places. For example, a miner made an interesting notation in his diary, writing: "Silver nugget weighing 397 pounds, 90% pure, make 8,212 silver dollars! Gold nugget from Lincoln, New Mexico Mine." This miner, or the person who wrote the notation, was claiming that he had found a fabulous and amazing silver nugget. Whatever the case, it is known that speculators tried every trick they could come up with to draw in people from the eastern states to turn a profit. They flimflammed gullible individuals, who believed they stood to strike it rich or own immense spreads of land by simply moving into New Mexico Territory and the West. Kansas was inundated with travelers, as reported in an edition of the *Evening Standard* newspaper published in Lawrence, Kansas, on February 16, 1878:

> *THE IMMIGRATION MOVEMENT. For months we have had intimations of the migration of large numbers of people from the East during the coming spring and summer, till every one has come to regard the movement for the season as of extraordinary extent, but it was not anticipated that it would commence as early as it has. Especially for the season of the year—midwinter in all the northerly portions of the country—the movement has suddenly assumed a magnitude that is simply astounding. The Kansas City papers report that for the past few days, all the railways have been crowded with land buyers and emigrants seeking new homes....On Thursday last about one thousand arrived at that place over the different roads. So great was the number that the roads running from there west and south, were not able to furnish cars for the people and their freight, consisting of livestock, household goods and farming implements. The eastern roads were obliged to put on special trains to accommodate them....The influx at the present time, from all sources, can hardly be less than a thousand a day, and if the present movement is any index to what is to be when at its height as spring*

New Mexico's Stolen Lands

Waterways were used by Americans for flourmills. Thomas D. Campbell, "Wheat King of New Mexico," paid the Socorro County Assessor's office thirty-five cents an acre for the La Joya Land Grant. *Photo by Ramón Juan Carlos de Aragón.*

comes on, and the facilities and season improve, it must in few weeks reach double that number. These people are scattering…very many are passing… along the Santa Fe and Kansas Pacific to the southwest and west.

The *Evening Standard* of Saturday, September 14, 1878, continued with a suggestion on the quickest way to make into the Territory of New Mexico: "'The Golden Belt' Route. The quickest, safest and most reliable route to all points East or west is via the Kansas Pacific railway, through the 'Golden Belt' the finest wheat region in the world….The Kansas Pacific fast freight express makes the best time and affords the most rapid transit of freight between the Missouri River and all principal points in…Colorado, New Mexico, San Juan, and Arizona."

At this time, the San Juan mining area was a part of the territory of New Mexico, which included most of Arizona and Colorado.

GOLD NUGGETS BY THE POUND—WILLIAM G. RITCH

William Gillett Ritch was born in Ulster County, New York, on May 4, 1830. During the Civil War, he served as a first lieutenant in the Forty-Sixth Volunteer Infantry Regiment of the Wisconsin Union Army. After the war, he served in the Wisconsin State Senate in 1868. Hearing about the vast opportunities available for both Union and Confederate veterans in the vast territory of New Mexico, he made his way to Santa Fe. Ritch rapidly fell in with the opportunists who had invaded the territory and quickly became friends with Tom B. Catron, the kingpin of the primary political Republican faction in the territory. William Ritch was named secretary of New Mexico Territory and, with the death of Governor Marsh Giddings on June 3, 1875, became acting governor until Samuel B. Axtell was appointed. He was an active member of the Knights Templar, a fraternal organization.

Secretary—later acting governor—Ritch's claim to fame was in promoting the wealth of New Mexico to tourists and American migrants. He wrote promotional material, including a booklet called *Aztlan: The History, Resources and Attractions of New Mexico*. Approximately one hundred thousand copies were printed and distributed. In a publication produced by the Bureau of Immigration at Santa Fe, New Mexico, in 1885, Ritch elaborated on the vast wealth that could be attained by moving into New Mexico,

> *From the New Placers have been taken some of the largest gold nuggets produced by the western hemisphere—the most valuable, eleven pounds nine ounces avoirdupois, was stumbled onto by a Pueblo Indian, and by him bartered away for a little whiskey, a blind pony and a crownless hat; another weighing more than $1,700, still another worth nearly $1,600, and several from that on down to the value of $1,000 and less. The encyclopedias corroborate the statements of rich finds in these placers....It is scarcely possible to wash a pan of dirt taken from anywhere in this vicinity* [Santa Fe] *without getting a color of gold. Recently a gentleman spent several days in this section testing, with a force of men, the placer ground, and his average for a scope of country six miles long, two miles deep, and at least forty feet deep, was a fraction over fifty-seven cents per cubic yard. What a world of wealth with water sufficient for extensive sluicing!*

New Mexico's Stolen Lands

The U.S. government confiscated millions of acres of common lands from grant owners, leased them to American cattle ranches and opened them up for American homesteading. *Photo by Ramón Juan Carlos de Aragón, 2002.*

Immigration Secretary Ritch was able to capitalize on an ancient Indian legend that recounted the history of Aztec origins with its golden temples and gold objects. As with any other oral history, legend is extremely difficult to separate from fact. Questions abound about whether or not a legend can be corroborated by evidence and how it will impact established beliefs. Modern-day scholars still contradict one another and argue about the legendary site of Aztlan. Ritch added that people could be drawn into the "last epoch of history, to be ushered in by the advent of ever restless and irresistible American, to whom has been reserved the gigantic task of developing the illimitable resources of this wonderful country, and by whom, eventually, the entire universe will be enriched in a most material manner."

He emphasized that any investment in the territory could yield upward of 70 to 100 percent in returns. He also assured Americans from the East that both the Indians and Mexicans residing in the territory could be easily subordinated, creating a pool of limitless workers for the mines and fields as well as riders and hands for ranchers.

Further appealing to American tourists to visit the city of Santa Fe, Ritch stated that they should especially pay a visit to Archbishop Lamy. With the American takeover of New Mexico, the pope in Rome appointed Jean

Baptiste Lamy as his vicariate apostolic, or bishop, of New Mexico Territory. Ritch informed American immigrants:

> *In Archbishop Lamy you will find a pleasant, elderly gentleman, a Frenchman by birth and education, tall and stately, who will kindly show you his garden and grounds, for which he feels a just pride. Briefly expressed, it is a most charming spot, cared for by French gardeners, having delightful walks, shady retreats, miniature lakes for fish, rippling water courses for irrigation, and which grows all the fruits and vegetables in season, adapted to the latitude and altitude. The "Bishop's Garden" is a most successful illustration of the grand adaptation to horticulture of the soil and climate of Santa Fe. Returning, His Grace will no doubt offer you a glass of native wine, and give you an opportunity to retire with pleasant impressions.... If you extend your trip out six miles to the Arroyo Hondo, you can find old pueblo ruins, and if you are enthusiastic enough to engage in excavating, you will no doubt be repaid with finds of archaeological remains.*

Immigration Secretary Ritch had a wild imagination, so much so that he created his own myths, supposedly drawn from ancient legends and folklore. He conveniently distorted actual facts and history to suit his needs. By these means, Ritch fabricated stories about the tremendous resources and opportunities available for Americans and others moving to New Mexico. He tied the mythical city of Aztlan, the place of origin of the Aztec golden empire, to New Mexico by saying:

> *There is a tradition of "Montezuma the great monarch," who is reputed to have said: "I command this province, which is the first of Aztlan, the pueblo of Teguayo, which governs one hundred and two pueblos. In this pueblo there is a great mine near by, in which they cut with stone hatchets the gold of my crown." At Santa Fe are to be found the remains of old smelters, with fragments of gold-bearing ore scattered about. Aztlan was near the portion of New Mexico and Arizona bounded by the 35th and 37th parallel of latitude....Rich mines are found in almost any direction... our mountains contain illimitable treasures, in the shape of lead, iron, copper, silver, mica and gold, and in the near future this beautiful country is destined to be known as the true El Dorado.*

HAPLESS HEROES

U.S. senator Dennis Chavez of New Mexico, in an *Albuquerque Journal* story published on January 1, 1944, appealed for tolerance, harmony and peace in America, as the new year dawned:

> *The New Year looms as one of momentous events and one, which will lie in the midst of the most crucial period in the history of the republic. Let us, as citizens of that still greater America which is to come, ponder deeply and sincerely the values of our form of Government as exemplified by our Declaration of Independence, our Constitution, and our Bill of Rights. Let us strain every sinew toward the prosecution of the principles of a pristine Americanism, unsoiled and unsullied by the evil forces of narrowness of mind, prejudice of heart and hypocrisy of spirit....The greatness of your America and mine is the issue of those lofty principles upon which our republic was founded; its greatness in the future will depend upon our will and determination to live together in harmony, in peace, and understanding. Let us project the spirit of the Christian tradition into the difficult years which lie ahead so that our children and our children's children may live under the comforts of God's physical and spiritual sunlight, and warmed also by that contentment of mind and spirit which can only flow from the practice of true Christian brotherhood....These are the words I offer my fellow Americans, in a spirit as humble as it is sincere, in the hope that they will constitute even a small contribution toward rebirth and practice of those principles for which men and women have laid down their lives across trying years of American history....Either we are all free, or we fail; democracy must belong to all of us.*

During World War II in New Mexico, older and disabled men who could not bear arms and fight were left behind. They, along with boys and girls, were forced to care for the farms and ranches, where work often took place from sunup to sundown. The women led at their homes and in the communities. They also mourned the loss of loved ones or, hopefully, waited for their return. Without surprise, these conditions were a boon for opportunists who saw another avenue to steal lands. There were bank foreclosures, properties sold for taxes and more barbed-wire fences being erected. Families were left at the mercy of manipulators. When many of the servicemen returned, they went back to lost lands or lands in the process of being lost. A case in point was the Tome Land Grant.

Disenchantment in New Mexico

After the Axis powers unconditionally surrendered on August 15, 1945, when the war ended in the Pacific and thus ended for good, those who survived returned to New Mexico. Some families lost all of their sons. Enrique Calles and his wife, Felicitas, who still lived on the land of their ancestors dating to the period when the first colonists entered New Mexico, were most fortunate. They embraced their sons: Elías, who had fought in France; José, who had been in the Philippines; and Adolfo, who had guarded German prisoners and carried wounded soldiers from ships to hospitals. Enrique was in his eighties and cared for his cattle, horses, pigs, turkeys, chickens, lambs and goats, which he raised on his ranch and farm while his sons were away. He also had grape vines and made wine to help supplement the family income. After the sons returned, they had to earn a living to support their own families.

Enrique Calles divided land among his sons. Since each was an heir of the Tome Land Grant, their livestock could graze on common lands. But they soon discovered that cattle and horses had been stolen on those lands. In fact, a Tome Land and Improvement Company Inc. was established, and heirs were given shares by the directors depending on how much improved land they owned. Shares were traded, and loans were secured on shares or bought and sold at local liquor stores. Some people gained a large number of shares to the land. As had happened throughout New Mexico, there were no longer communal grazing lands or communal watering areas. The Middle Rio Grande Conservancy District, a state agency, now controlled how water was used and distributed throughout the Rio Grande Valley. In New Mexico, land grants were converted into private corporations to help manage land grant assets. In 1967, the New Mexico state legislature allowed these corporations, established in 1891, to reorganize as for-profit stock corporations that could develop the land

World War II veteran Elías Calles poses proudly with his uniform. He, along with brothers José and Adolfo, also veterans, were victims of land grant theft after the war. *Author's collection.*

grants and pay dividends to the heirs and shareholders, as would later be established by New Mexico courts.

The Tome Land Grant Company, through its board of directors, sold around fifty thousand acres. From the proceeds of the sale, amounting to several millions of dollars, each grantee was given from $7,000 to $15,000, as determined by their proven chain of succession. After various claimants who said they had been excluded from the sale filed several lawsuits, the Supreme Court of the State of New Mexico ordered that the district court "redetermine heir-ship and redistribute funds realized from the sale to Horizon Corporation," which had purchased the lands. Those original direct heirs were forced to return funds paid to them under the threat of liens to be filed against their land properties and personal property. "In furtherance of that Order, the District Court has now been determined that there are more than 3,500 'heirs,' and has hired two Albuquerque attorneys to begin collection procedures." In an extension of public announcements, it was claimed that the sale was illegal, because it was a community land grant, but the purchase was legal, because the purchasers bought the land in good faith.

Needless to say, since thousands of claimants from all parts of the country now said they were heirs, by the time the courts settled the issue and each claimant was wanting to receive moneys from the proceeds, all new claimants received little money while the originally determined 395 heirs to the Tome Land Grant who had received the original disbursement got nothing, due to "Judgments by Default." Many lawyers were involved in this case and millions of dollars were spent on attorney fees. These lawyers became well off and successful, while actual heirs and their immediate families not only suffered loss of land but had to borrow money from banks in order to avoid the threat of liens on their homes.

CRIME AND PUNISHMENT

In 1967, New Mexico governor David Cargo, after returning to the New Mexico state capital from a trip to Michigan, exclaimed: "We came over Santa Fe. You could look down La Bajada Hill. As I looked down, I saw all these army tanks and trucks, and I thought, what in the hell is going on here?"

Injustices were taking place in New Mexico against the people, and many voices were heard. Reies López Tijerina spoke out and said the people were guaranteed the rights to the lands in the Treaty of Guadalupe Hidalgo,

Disenchantment in New Mexico

On October 12, 1971, Reies López Tijerina delivered a passionate and fiery speech at New Mexico Highlands University. He decried land loss and theft. *Author's collection.*

which had ended the Mexican-American War. He declared, "Es una chispa del espíritu que nos va a mover. El tratado es una vergüenza, una desgracia, y un escandalo!" ("It is a spark of the spirit that will move us. The treaty is an embarrassment, a disgrace and a scandal!")

On June 5, 1967, all hell broke out in Tierra Amarilla, New Mexico. This event made national and international news as the famous "Tierra Amarilla Courthouse Raid." The New Mexico National Guard was quickly activated, and Major General John P. Jolly deployed troops and sent tanks and armored vehicles into the small, sleepy town of Tierra Amarilla. The New Mexico Air National Guard at Kirtland Air Force Base with its squadron of fighter jets was placed on alert. The panic sweeping New Mexico about Reies López Tijerina and his land grant organization, La Alianza de Las Mercedes, had its basis in publications produced by radical American groups. Alan Stang, a former business editor for Prentice-Hall Inc. and a television writer, producer and consultant, was one who spent a great deal of time stirring things up. In a publication called *American Opinion* published in 1969, Stang equated Tijerina and other civil rights activists with communists.

FRIDAY, the thirteenth, is said to be unlucky, and it is. On Friday, December 13, 1968, a jury in Albuquerque acquitted Castroite terrorist Reies Tijerina of kidnapping, false imprisonment, and assault on a jail—crimes committed when he led an armed guerilla raid against the Rio Arriba County Courthouse on June 5, 1967. (See AMERICAN OPINION, *October, 1967.)...On the other side of the rail sat Tijerina's attorneys. They included Beverly Axelrod, a conspirator and former fiancée of Eldrige Cleaver, Minister of Information of the communist Black Panther Party and a fugitive from justice....And there was Reies' man William L. Higgs, who has also represented agitator James Meredith, and who entered the courtroom shirt unbuttoned and tie askew, his clothes literally streaked with dirt....Higgs by the way is, white and a gringo.... The victorious Tijerina was later quoted (*New York Times, *December 22, 1968) as follows: The cricket had no chance against the lion, so he jumped into the lion's ear and tickled him to death. That's what we're going to do to the United States—we're going to tickle him to death....Crucial to all Communist activity in New Mexico is the famous San Cristobal Valley Ranch, about twenty miles north of Taos, in the heart of the territory Reies Tijerina is terrorizing....As for Reies Lopez Tijerina himself, he has been busy revolting during the past year as you would expect. In the summer of 1968, he was a leader of the Communist "Poor People's March" in Washington....Others involved in local agitation include attorney William J. Fitzpatrick, of the legal Aid Society...attorney Paul A. Phillips, head of the local American Civil Liberties Union—founded primarily by Communist Harry F. Ward...and Mrs. Helen H. Ellis, Social Consultant of the Unitarian Church....He (Reies) expected all of his followers to vote for Republican David Cargo. You will remember that Mrs. Cargo has been a member of Tijerina's organization and that the Governor has run interference for Tijerina....Reies of course has become a hot cargo— red hot....His real identity remains unknown. You will remember the demonstration; in my earlier article on the affair that no proof exists that he was born in the United States. Since then, interested police officials in various places and agencies have unsuccessfully asked for help of the U.S. Department of Immigration and Naturalization in this matter. To no avail! A source close to Tijerina now tells us, however, that in 1961 or 1962, Reies went to Cuba, where he met with Communist dictator Fidel Castro; and that among things Reies says Castro gave him a Chinese manual on guerrilla warfare....So there it is. Incredible though it may be—and it is incredible—a Castroite guerilla war is being arranged for the American Southwest. Reies Tijerina, or whomever it is who gives the orders, may already have selected a day this spring or summer as Der Tag.*

Disenchantment in New Mexico

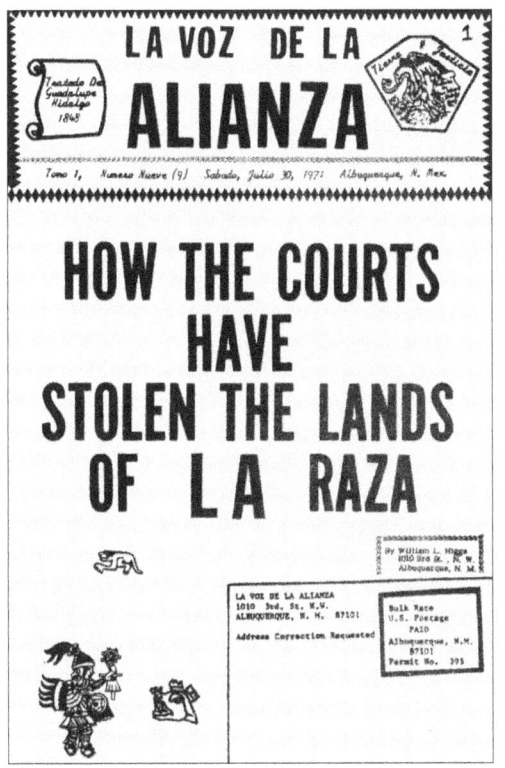

La Voz de la Alianza (the voice of the alliance). Tijerina's periodical kept people informed as to the land grant movement and its progress. *Author's collection.*

Jack Stamm, reporter for the *New Mexican*, a Santa Fe newspaper, quoted a district attorney as saying in 1968,

> Members of the Alianza...reportedly are being trained in guerrilla warfare tactics in Communist Clubs and on a ranch in Taos....They are importing known communists into its organization from Mexico....Most of these people are not interested in owning the National Forest. They only want to graze their animals on it. They can't afford to pay taxes on it....A few years ago there was a rash of haystack burnings to do with the other political reasons that had motivated burnings for the past one hundred years....

The issues involving theft of land grants in New Mexico were not new. The struggle had been taking place for generations. In fact, territorial officials, state officials, and later elected officials in the congress and senate attempted to bring the plight of the people to the attention of others. Congressman Antonio Manuel Fernandez of New Mexico was one of many who strived to get something done about rampant land theft in New Mexico.

NEW MEXICO'S STOLEN LANDS

Impoverished families tried to survive after losing farms, ranches and livestock to land swindlers. *Unknown photographer, circa 1930. Author's collection.*

Antonio Manuel Fernandez (1902–1956) served in the U.S. Congress from 1943 to 1956. He was the longest-serving representative from New Mexico. The Springer, New Mexico native was appointed to the committees of Public Lands, Indian Affairs, Insular Affairs, Mines and Mining, Veterans Affairs and others. In an address to Congress, Fernandez emphasized the sacrifices and bravery of New Mexico Hispanic and Indian servicemen during World War II and talked about the Bataan Death March. He also spoke about the impoverished and destitute Navajo and Hopi Indians. The phenomenal role of the Navajo Code Talkers is well documented. Coming from northern New Mexico, Congressman Fernandez was well aware of the plight and the suffering experienced by land grant heirs. On May 12, 1942, Fernandez made the following remarks at a session of the proceedings and debates of the Seventy-Eighth Congress, Second Session 4162:

> *In the great press of work which year after year is brought before the Congress by the stress of problems as old as the hills unavoidably remain unnoticed in the background until small voices of those affected, like a*

cry in the wilderness, make but little or no impression....Such is the fate of a large number of old families in the State of New Mexico who, if they remain unheeded and their problems unattended, will in the not-too-distant future end in calamity....I want to give you some of the facts, in connection with a bill which I have introduced—a bill conveying certain lands to the children of children of the first settlers thereon and who through the years in good faith have believed that they have had no title from this Government despite the good intentions of our nation as expressed in the Treaty of Guadalupe Hidalgo....Under that treaty, this Government undertook to protect fully the rights of the then settlers of what became the Territory of New Mexico. In carrying out that intention in good faith, the Congress recognized and confirmed various Spanish and Mexican land grants to individuals and to communities as such. Between 1854 and 1870 the Congress confirmed some sixty-two grants...among these was the claim of a group of families established in Rio Arriba County, in New Mexico, under Spanish Grant prior to Mexican rule and American sovereignty. The Spanish Government had set aside, for these families and their descendants, a huge tract of land known by direction of

American speculators and homesteaders arriving in New Mexico Territory were stunned by the beauty of the land and its richness. They wanted it. *Photo by James Furlong, 1879. Author's collection.*

the granting authority itself as the "San Joaquin del Rio Chama." Under this claim, known as Land Claim No. 71, the Department of the Interior through the Surveyor-General, made a survey of the grant in 1878, and the survey was approved, submitted to the Congress, and the committee on Public Lands reported out a bill confirming the grant to them.... Through intricacies the Government later took over the land and claimed it as its own.... The fact of the matter is that the grant was not confirmed... but that it was relegated to a newly established Court of Private Land claims—taken there by the action of certain interests who claimed, as so many did in those days, an alleged purchase of the trust from the people.... The Court of Private Land Claims refusing to recognize anything but small patches on which the homes and small cultivated pieces were located, and to recognize none of the land used for grazing and held in common under immemorial policy of the preceding government, approved only 1,422.62 acres.... The Supreme Court of the United States affirmed the case, brought not by the grantees, but by a land and cattle company, stating that under the law of its creation it could recognize no vesting of title in the community to common lands but only to the individual allotments assigned to each individual in severalty.... Those families, heirs and descendants... continued for years in undisturbed possession in the belief that the lands they grazed—and on several portions of which there growing family

A destitute New Mexico family built a ramshackle shack from scrap material after being evicted from their land. *Unknown photographer and date. Author's collection.*

groups had established additional communities—belonged to them.... When the Federal Government finally exercised its domain over the land, those poor families, appealing to lawyers for help, and without funds to finance an intelligent investigation have been met with a firm denial of assistance in the belief that this case settled the matter once and forever....I cannot agree that it did, I cannot agree that this Government is without authority and without desire to do justice in the premises, and I believe this Congress upon investigation will feel as I do....When and if the Congress does...investigate...all the history of the San Joaquin del Rio de Chama communities...we shall whatever the result is, be satisfied. But those good people whose sons fought in the Spanish-American War, in the First World War and in this war, and numbers of whose sons are now prisoners of war in the hands of the Japanese, will never, never feel satisfied unless and until this Government of ours does pay heed to their petition for redress and does look into all the facts with patience and sympathetic understanding.

COURTS, BANKS AND TRUSTS

New Mexico went from an agrarian culture to an urban society during the decade of the 1940s. On May 8, 1790, a portion of land two hundred varas wide (a unit of linear measurement varying from thirty-four inches to forty-four inches, more or less) from north to south and two hundred varas wide from east to west was excluded from the original Nicolás Duran y Chávez Grant. The land ran west to the Rio Puerco several miles in length and width. This large tract of land eventually fell into the hands of Doña Bárbara Chávez de Sánchez, the third great-granddaughter of Nicolás Duran y Chávez, whose grant was patented in 1896 by the U.S. government for 46,200.94 acres. To help secure her claim to the land, Doña Bárbara filed for a homestead of 640 acres, and she was granted the homestead on land she already owned. Deeds were recorded from Doña Bárbara passing her lands on to her son Ignacio Colombo Sánchez.

The 1790s land was conveyed to Ignacio on December 19, 1914. Lucia de Aragón (1892–1938), Doña Bárbara's granddaughter and Ignacio's niece, was deeded the tract of land on March 25, 1925, and property taxes were continued to be faithfully paid. Lucia de Aragón from Las Vegas, New Mexico, was a highly recognized ballet dancer in New York City who owned properties in New York; downtown Denver, Colorado; downtown Albuquerque, New Mexico; and Las Vegas, New Mexico. She also became sole owner of the Las Salinas Grant and the New Mexico Salt Refining Company, and she was a direct descendant and heir of the Duran y Chávez Grant. She was proclaimed the "Baroness of New Mexico" in a story about her life. A special master settled Lucia de Aragón's estate after her untimely death on May 5, 1938, from an aneurism.

A corporation known as the Nicolás Duran y Chávez Grant Company was organized by a group of investors. They made purchases of lands in the Nicolás Duran y Chávez Land Grant. A proxy was hired to secure powers of attorney from the original heirs "to help them secure their claims to the land." The proxy later transferred the powers of attorney to the Nicolás Duran y Chávez Land Grant Company. In an attempt to quiet title to the land that was exempted from the original land grant, Maximo de Aragón, an heir with a clear chain of title, filed suit to quiet title to the land of his great-grandmother Bárbara Chávez de Sánchez. Valencia County district judge H. Vern Payne without hesitation ruled in favor of the opposing Anglo parties. The judge's statement was to the effect that everyone believed that all of the Nicolás Duran y Chávez Grant was originally involved in initial land grant sales; therefore, this land situated in the Village of Los Chavez, near Los Lunas, New Mexico, should have also been included. The district judge then asked the opposition attorneys if there was anything else he could do for them. It was later discovered that de Aragón's attorney, who was also associated with Sun West Bank and Trust as an official, received ten acres of choice land for withdrawing support of his client and siding with the other parties. H. Vern Payne was appointed a New Mexico Supreme Court justice.

In a story for *Natural Resources Journal*, Judge H. Vern Payne wrote: "As the economy of New Mexico continues to expand, lawyers will be called upon to handle more and more problems dealing with secured financing. Some of these problems will no doubt involve competing claims between those holding security interests in personal property and those with interests in real property."

A newspaper story carried in the *Albuquerque Journal* dated May 16, 2008, had a story about dubious land fraud. *Journal* investigative reporter Colleen Heild wrote that Pat Owens, general manager/partner of Cypress Estates in Valencia County in New Mexico, accused those of being involved with the land deals, were embroiled in theft. She was quoted as saying, "This is the most egregious act of fraud, deceit, concealment, and thievery imaginable." It was reported that an elderly group of investors was involved in millions of dollars in transactions for 552 residential lots in Valencia County in Los Chavez near Los Lunas. Payne and a client named Tom Wilson were both sued as a result. Sun West Trust was listed as a defendant. Checks written by Payne provided Wilson with over $1 million that he used to lavish himself with personal purchases. H. Vern Payne, who had returned to private practice from his stint as a Supreme Court justice, deducted his attorney's fees and affirmed that he was not actively involved in any unethical practices. Payne advertised his practice as a land attorney and expert.

In October 2006, Tom Wilson was arrested in Albuquerque on a fugitive warrant related to felony, vehicle theft and fraud by check. He had also been charged in Gunnison County, Colorado, for embezzlement. Wilson had also been sued for securities fraud in New York by a group of real estate partners. He was arrested by the New Mexico State Police in Albuquerque but was taken to the Heart Hospital after he complained of severe chest pains. Wilson immediately filed for bankruptcy on advice of his counsel. This effectively halted legal proceedings against him until the bankruptcy could be resolved.

Derek Lancer, in a story called "Walking between Rain Drops," wrote about Thomas Clay Wilson Sr.: "Is he the most brilliant conman in US history? This guy makes the characters in *Dirty Rotten Scoundrels* look like Boy Scouts earning merit badges...Wilson cannot be touched for his heinous acts because 'he knows all the holes in the legal system and is made of 100% Teflon' according to scam victim Patricia Owens who lost a reported 1.6 million dollars in New Mexico....Perhaps one day congress will pass the Thomas Clay Sr. Scam Prevention Act."

Judge H. Vern Payne, Wilson's legal counsel, had already left his mark on New Mexico history by sentencing civil rights and land grant rights activist Reies López Tijerina to two years in prison for destruction of Kit Carson National Forest property by purportedly vandalizing forest signs. Tijerina maintained his innocence to the end. A former jury while reviewing his reported involvement had previously found Reies Tijerina innocent in the famous Tierra Amarilla Courthouse Raid. This time, he was in front of a well-known judge who selectively dispensed land justice, as his peers had done historically. An application filed by H. Vern Payne for a State of New Mexico Domestic Professional Corporation on October 22, 1999, is listed as "Revoked Final."

It is now written that the Zoot Suit Riots and the hysteria of the 1940s was a symbol of cultural resistance that spawned the "Chicano Movement" of the 1960s and 1970s. A struggle for civil rights swept the nation. Black Americans led by Dr. Martin Luther King Jr.; Mexican American farmworkers directed by Cesar Chávez; and, in New Mexico, the Alianza Land Grant struggles with social justice fighter Reies López Tijerina and his followers gained national and international attention. Unfortunately, land rights struggles before New Mexico courts remain to the present day.

> *Government to them is made up of people who only abuse them, never help them. If you could pave roads with broken promises we would have blacktopped all of northern New Mexico years ago....In Rio Arriba the OEO provided programs both of Head Start and of frustration, because they spent more time counting outhouses than counting people....There is little chance for education, poverty, poor roads, disputes over park boundaries and the people being refused permits to graze cattle in the national forest; all are conditions that led to the courthouse raid.*
> —David F. Cargo

BIBLIOGRAPHY

FURTHER READING AND PRIMARY SOURCES

Álvarez, Simón, and Gonzales, Eddie T. *Reies López Tijerina—Héroe de los Pueblos, Tijerina, Hero of the People.* Albuquerque, NM: Longfellow Elementary School, 1977.
Arellano, Anselmo F. *The Never-Ending Land Grant Struggle.* Austin: University of Texas, n.d.
Bloom, John Porter, ed. *The Treaty of Guadalupe Hidalgo, 1848: Papers of the Sesquicentennial Symposium.* Las Cruces, NM: Dona Ana County.
Bradfute, Richard Wells. *The Court of Private Land Claims: Adjudication of Spanish and Mexican Land Grant Titles, 1841–1904.* Albuquerque: University of New Mexico Press, 1975.
Brayer, Herbert O. *Pueblo Indian Land Grants of the "Rio Abajo."* Albuquerque: University of New Mexico Press, 1939.
Briggs, Charles L., and John R. Van Ness, eds. *Land, Water, and Culture: New Perspectives on Hispanic Land Grants.* Albuquerque: University of New Mexico Press, 1987.
Cabeza de Baca, Vincent. *La Gente: Hispano History and Life in Colorado.* Denver: Historical Society of Colorado, 1998.
Chavez, Fray Angelico, and Thomas E. Chavez. *Wake for a Fat Vicar.* Albuquerque, NM: LPD Press, 2004.
Cookridge, E.H., *The Baron of Arizona.* New York: Ballantine Books, 1972.
De Aragón, Ray John. "El Conciliador: Resumen de la Vida del Padre Antonio Jose Martinez." *El Hispano,* July 1975.

Bibliography

———. "El Padre Martinez y el Obispo Lamy." *La Luz Magazine*, April 1972.
———. *Haunted Santa Fe*. Charleston, SC: The History Press, 2018.
———. *Hidden History of Spanish New Mexico*. Charleston, SC: The History Press, 2012.
———. "Mora Intrigue and Murder." *New Mexico Magazine*, August 1982.
———. *Padre Martinez and Bishop Lamy*. Las Vegas, NM: Pan American Publishing, 1976.
———. "Padre Martinez Memory Scarred." *El Hispano*, June 1978.
———. *Padre Martinez: New Perspectives from Taos*. Taos, NM: Millicent Rogers Museum, 1988.
Diario de Gobierno. *Plan of Tome, October 19, 1837*. Santa Fe, NM: State Records Center and Archives, n.d.
Diaz, Albert James. *A Guide to the Microfilm of Papers Relating to New Mexico Land Grants*. Albuquerque: University of New Mexico Press, 1960.
Ellis, Richard N., ed. *New Mexico Historic Documents*. Albuquerque: University of New Mexico Press, 1975.
Espinosa, Gilberto. "New Mexico Land Grants." *State Bar of New Mexico Journal* 1, no. 2 (1962): 3–13.
Hall, G. Emlen. "San Miguel del Bado and the Loss of the Common Lands of New Mexico Community Land Grants." *New Mexico Historical Review* 66 (October 1991): 413–32.
Kessell, John L. *Kiva, Cross, and Crown: The Pecos Indians of New Mexico 1540–1840*. Albuquerque: University of New Mexico Press, 1987.
Knowlton, Clark S. *Land-Grant Problems among the State's Spanish Americans*. Unpublished and undated paper, University of Texas.
Kutche, Paul, and John R. Van Ness. *Canones—Values, Crisis, and Survival in a Northern New Mexico Village*. Albuquerque: University of New Mexico Press, 1981.
Leonard, Olen E. *The Role of the Land Grant in the Social Organization and Social Processes of a Spanish-American Village in New Mexico*. Albuquerque: Calvin Horn, 1970.
Lowie, Robert H. *Indians of the Plains*. Garden City, NY: Natural History Press, 1962.
Martínez, Elizabeth, ed. *500 Years of Chicano History in Pictures*. Albuquerque, NM: Southwest Organizing Project (SWOP), 1991.
McCarty, Frankie. "Land Grant Problems in New Mexico." *Albuquerque Journal*, September 28–October 10, 1969.

Mexican Archives of New Mexico. *Microfilm Publication of the New Mexico State Records Center and Archives*, Roll 42, Legislative Records.

Nostrand, Richard L. *The Hispano Homeland*. Norman: University of Oklahoma Press, 1992.

Perrigo, Lynn I. *Hispanos-Historic Leaders in New Mexico*. Santa Fe, NM: Sunstone Press, 1985.

Powell, Donald M. *The Peralta Grant: James Addison Reavis and the Barony of Arizona*. Norman: University of Oklahoma Press, 1960.

Reeve, Frank D. *History of New Mexico*. 2 vols. New York: Lewis Historical Publishing, 1961.

Rosenbaum, Robert J. *Mexicano Resistance in the Southwest "The Sacred Right of Self-Preservation."* Austin: University of Texas Press, 1981.

Tyler, Daniel. *Sources for New Mexican History 1821–1848*. Santa Fe: Museum of New Mexico Press, 1984.

Westphall, Victor. "Fraud and Implications of Fraud in the Land Grants of New Mexico." *New Mexico Historical Review* 49, no. 3 (1974): 189–218.

———. *Thomas Benton Catron and His Era*. Tucson: University of Arizona Press, 1973.

ABOUT THE AUTHOR

Ray John de Aragón became an active member of La Alianza Federal de las Mercedes in May 1967. This was a land grant organization founded by civil rights activist Reies López Tijerina. His goal was to have millions of acres of Spanish/Mexican land grants returned to their rightful owners as heirs. Tijerina also fought for the rights of Native Americans who had lost their ancestral lands. Reies became a controversial figure along with his compatriots Dr. Martin Luther King Jr. and Cesar Chávez. They all had a dream that justice would prevail. Ray John remains actively involved, not only speaking out on issues that affect downtrodden people but also following up by prolifically writing about these issues.

www.ingramcontent.com/pod-product-compliance
Lightning Source LLC
Chambersburg PA
CBHW040251170426
43191CB00018B/2377

www.ingramcontent.com/pod-product-compliance
Lightning Source LLC
Chambersburg PA
CBHW040251170426
43191CB00018B/2376